WALKING IN THE CHILTERNS

About the Author

Steve Davison is a freelance writer and photographer who has spent 30 years walking in the Thames Valley region. He has written several guidebooks as well as articles for a number of outdoor magazines and national and local newspapers, specialising in hill-walking and UK and European travel, and counts nature, geology and the countryside among his particular interests. A keen hill-walker for many years, and a Mountain Leader, Steve has also worked as a part-time outdoor education instructor. He is also a member of the Outdoor Writers and Photographers Guild. Find out more about him at www.steve-davison.co.uk

Other Cicerone guides by the author
Walking the Kennet and Avon Canal
Walking the Great Stones Way
Walking in the North Wessex Downs
Walking The Ridgeway National Trail
Walking in the New Forest
Walking in the Thames Valley

WALKING IN THE CHILTERNS

by Steve Davison

JUNIPER HOUSE, MURLEY MOSS,
OXENHOLME ROAD, KENDAL, CUMBRIA LA9 7RL
www.cicerone.co.uk

Printed by China on behalf of Latitude Press Ltd.
A catalogue record for this book is available from the British Library.
All photographs are by the author unless otherwise stated.

Updates to this Guide

While every effort is made by our authors to ensure the accuracy of guidebooks as they go to print, changes can occur during the lifetime of an edition. Any updates that we know of for this guide will be on the Cicerone website (www.cicerone.co.uk/1018/updates), so please check before planning your trip. We also advise that you check information about such things as transport, accommodation and shops locally. Even rights of way can be altered over time. We are always grateful for information about any discrepancies between a guidebook and the facts on the ground, sent by email to updates@cicerone.co.uk or by post to Cicerone, Juniper House, Murley Moss, Oxenholme Road, Kendal, LA9 7RL.

Register your book: To sign up to receive free updates, special offers and files where available, register your book at www.cicerone.co.uk.

Front cover: Typical Chiltern scenery on the way to Christmas Common (Walk 22)

CONTENTS

Map key 6
Overview map 7

INTRODUCTION 9
Geology 10
Plants and wildlife 12
Brief history 14
Where to stay 16
Getting to and around the Chilterns 16
Food and drink 17
Walking in the Chilterns 18
Maps 19
Waymarking, access and rights of way 20
Using this guide 21

1 NORTH OF LUTON 23
Walk 1   Harlington and Sharpenhoe Clappers 24
Walk 2   Barton-le-Clay, Hexton and Barton Hills 29
Walk 3   Pirton and Pegsdon Hills 35

2 DUNSTABLE TO BERKHAMSTED 41
Walk 4   Whipsnade, Studham and the Dunstable Downs 42
Walk 5   Ivinghoe Beacon, Ivinghoe and Pitstone 48
Walk 6   Grand Union Canal, Pitstone Hill and Aldbury 53
Walk 7   Grand Union Canal and Tring Park 57
Walk 8   Great Gaddesden 62
Walk 9   Berkhamsted, Nettleden and Little Gaddesden 67

3 WENDOVER TO STOKENCHURCH 73
Walk 10   Cholesbury and Hawridge 74
Walk 11   Wendover and The Lee 78
Walk 12   Wendover, Ellesborough, Chequers and Coombe Hill 85
Walk 13   Whiteleaf Hill and Great Kimble 90
Walk 14   Bledlow and Radnage 95
Walk 15   Lacey Green, Speen and Bryant's Bottom 101
Walk 16   Great Hampden 106
Walk 17   Great Missenden and Chartridge 110

4 AMERSHAM TO HIGH WYCOMBE 117
Walk 18   Chenies, Latimer and the River Chess 118
Walk 19   Little Missenden, Penn Wood and Penn Street 123
Walk 20   Hughenden, Bradenham and West Wycombe 128
Walk 21   Penn and Coleshill 133

5 WATLINGTON AND NETTLEBED 139
Walk 22   Christmas Common and Watlington Hill 140
Walk 23   Turville, Skirmett and Fingest 145
Walk 24   Pishill and Stonor 150
Walk 25   Pishill, Cookley Green and Russell's Water 155
Walk 26   Ewelme and Swyncombe 160
Walk 27   Checkendon and Stoke Row 165
Walk 28   Hailey and Grim's Ditch 170
Walk 29   Nettlebed and Nuffield 173
Walk 30   Greys Green, Rotherfield Greys and Greys Court 179

6 ALONG THE THAMES 183
Walk 31   Hambleden, Medmenham and the River Thames 184
Walk 32   Henley-on-Thames and Middle Assendon 190
Walk 33   South and North Stoke and Grim's Ditch 197
Walk 34   Goring-on-Thames and Cray's Pond 205
Walk 35   Whitchurch Hill and Mapledurham 211

Appendix A   Route summary table 216
Appendix B   Useful contacts 218

Route symbols on OS map extracts

For OS legend see printed OS maps

 route

alternative/detour/shortcut

 start/finish point

 alternative
start/finish point

◄ direction of walk

The extracts from 1:50,000 OS maps
used in this book have been reproduced
at 1:40,000 for greater clarity

GPX files for all routes can be downloaded free at www.cicerone.co.uk/1018/GPX.

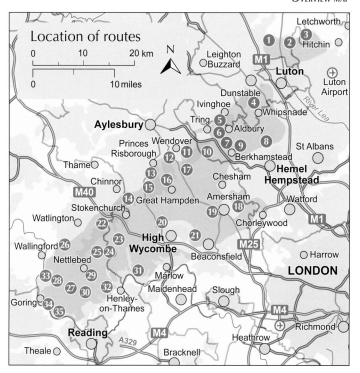

Location of routes

Features on the overview map

—— County/Unitary boundary

Urban area

The Chilterns Area of
Outstanding Natural Beauty

400m
200m
75m
0m

Leaving Great Chalk Wood to head through fields towards Goring-on-Thames (Walk 34)

INTRODUCTION

Looking north from Pitstone Hill (Walk 6) to Steps Hill (straight ahead) and Ivinghoe Beacon (left) – visited on Walk 5

The Chilterns Area of Outstanding Natural Beauty (AONB) covers an area of 833km² in south-east England, stretching north-east for 70km from the River Thames at the Goring Gap in Oxfordshire through Buckinghamshire and Bedfordshire to Hertfordshire. This chalk landscape is famed for its beech and oak woods (around one fifth of the area is covered by woodland) which give way to a more open chalk grassland along its northern reaches, such as the Ivinghoe Hills and Dunstable Downs. The Chilterns are definitely 'hilly' but they don't rise to any great height: the highest point – albeit a rather indistinct feature surrounded by dense woodland – is Haddington Hill near Wendover at 267m. More prominent hills, with the advantage of panoramic views, include Coombe Hill near Wendover at 260m (Walk 12) and Beacon Hill near Ivinghoe at 249m (Walk 5).

The area of the AONB itself has a relatively low population – around 100,000 – but its boundary skirts around larger urban areas such as High Wycombe and Luton, meaning that a further half million people live within 3km. Good transport links also make the Chilterns easily accessible to people from London.

Yet peace and tranquillity are in abundance: listen to the birdsong in the ancient woodlands or the skylarks singing over the open grassland; be dazzled by the myriad flowers and butterflies; admire the gently rolling landscape that has inspired many over the centuries, from famed authors to artists and poets, including the WWI poet Rupert Brookes, who wrote of the countryside in his poem *The Chilterns*:

I shall desire and I shall find
The best of my desires;
The autumn road, the mellow wind
That soothes the darkening shires.
And laughter, and inn-fires.

Be inspired, and explore some of the 2000km of footpaths and bridleways that criss-cross the Chilterns.

GEOLOGY

The geology of the Chilterns tells the story of the seas that once covered southern England and the sediments that were laid down at that time. It is perhaps easiest to think of the area's geological structure as a multi-layered cake.

The lowest, and oldest, layers of this 'cake' in the Chilterns are formed from Gault Clay and Upper Greensand, laid down during the latter part of the Lower Cretaceous period (145–99 million years ago). In the middle is a thick layer of Upper Cretaceous chalk, formed 99–65 million years ago from incredible numbers of minute calcareous shells which are the remains of plankton, known as coccoliths, which lived in the shallow subtropical seas that

Looking north along the crest of the Dunstable Downs to the summit above Pascomb Pit (Walk 4)

St Mary's Church, Hawridge – a typical flint-built church (Walk 10)

once covered much of southern England.

Chalk is a highly porous rock with numerous microscopic pore spaces that can store huge amounts of water, thus it acts like a giant sponge or aquifer, soaking up most of the rainfall. Because of this, over most of the higher ground there is no surface water in the form of ponds or streams.

Associated mainly with the upper (white) layer of chalk are horizontal bands of irregular silica concretions, known as flints; these also occur in profusion in the jumbled deposits of weathered chalk, known as 'clay-with-flints'. When struck, flint breaks with a shell-shaped fracture, leaving very sharp edges, and our Stone Age ancestors used flints to make a range of tools. Being a very hard-wearing rock, flint has been widely used as a building material both in its natural state and knapped to form a flatter surface. It is a characteristic of the area – a great number of the region's churches and old cottages have flint walls.

Finally, at the top are the Tertiary (65–2.6 million year-old) deposits that include layers of clay. Historically this clay has been used to make bricks and tiles, such as at Nettlebed (Walk 29). It was during the Tertiary period that the European and African continental plates collided – an event that formed the Alps. In southern England the effects were less dramatic, although the collision caused our sedimentary 'cake' to ripple, with resultant changes to the landscape that remain in evidence today, including the formation of a prominent ridge with a steep north-facing scarp slope along the northern edge of the Chilterns with the wide, flat plain of the Vale of Aylesbury beyond. This rippled layer of chalk also forms the Berkshire Downs, the North Hampshire Downs, the North and South Downs and the Purbeck Hills in Dorset.

Throughout the last 2.6 million years (the Quaternary period) Britain has been subject to periods of glaciation separated by warmer interglacial periods (the last glacial period ended about 12,000 years ago). During these glacial periods much of Britain was hidden beneath a thick layer of ice. There is no evidence to suggest that the Chilterns were ever covered in ice, but the area did suffer periglacial conditions which allowed the formation of dry valleys, or coombes, in the chalk plateau, eroded by water flowing over the surface of the chalk during cold periods when the underlying ground was frozen, making the normally porous chalk impermeable.

Another major feature caused by glaciation was the creation of the Goring Gap and the diversion of the Thames southwards to flow past Reading. Originally the river flowed through the Vale of St Albans, past Watford and Hertford, eventually reaching the North Sea in East Anglia near Ipswich. The gap was created when a large glacial lake, which formed over the Oxford area about 450,000 years ago, eroded a line of weakness in the chalk. The Goring Gap now forms a junction between the Chiltern Hills to the east and the Berkshire Downs to the west.

PLANTS AND WILDLIFE

The Chilterns form a patchwork landscape with areas of broadleaved woodland (especially beech and oak), open chalk grassland and farmland. Many of the wooded areas are known as ancient woodlands, having been continuously wooded since at least 1600. These areas tend to support a greater number of species as their character often closely reflects the underlying soil conditions, producing a wide range of woodland types and wildlife habitats.

Below the downs, chalk streams flow from the spring-line that forms along the boundary between the upper porous chalk and a lower impervious layer of Gault Clay, resulting in water that has seeped through the porous layer being forced to the surface. Chalk streams support a diversity of plant and animal life; some of these streams, such as the Hamble Brook (Walk 31), are winterbournes, only appearing after heavy winter rainfall.

Throughout the Chilterns you should have plenty of opportunity to catch glimpses of local wildlife, from foxes to roe and fallow deer or the much smaller muntjac; you may even catch sight of the elusive badger

Red Kite (milvus milvus) – a fairly common sight throughout much of the Chilterns

as dusk approaches, or an edible dormouse around Tring Park (Walk 7). Alongside the streams and rivers, as well as seeing the ever-present ducks and mute swans, you may spot the vivid turquoise-blue-and-orange flash of a kingfisher as it darts along the river, or an otter, or the endangered water vole.

In the ancient broadleaved woodlands – which are carpeted in late spring and early summer with vivid bluebells – you may hear the drumming knock of the great spotted woodpecker declaring its territory, or the raucous call of a jay; those with a keen eye might catch sight of a goldcrest or nuthatch.

The open chalk grasslands support a wide range of butterflies, plants (including gentians and orchids) and birds such as the pheasant, skylark and yellowhammer.

High above you might see the majestic silhouette of a buzzard, or hear the high-pitched whistling call – 'weeoo-wee-weewee' – of a red kite. Buzzards have broader wings and a rounded tail, while red kites have a distinctive forked tail and chestnut-red plumage. The latter were successfully reintroduced between 1989 and 1994 and their numbers have steadily increased.

Anyone wishing to identify the flora and fauna they see while out

Clockwise from left: Cowslip (Primula Veris), Clustered Bellflower (Campanula Glomerata) and Common Spotted Orchid (Dactylohiza Fuschii)

walking should carry a guidebook and a pair of binoculars.

BRIEF HISTORY

Around 12,000 years ago the last Ice Age was coming to an end; the climate was warming and both people and animals migrated northwards from mainland Europe before the formation of the English Channel made Britain an island for the last time. The hunter-gatherer lifestyle flourished, and by the start of the Neolithic period (4200—2200BC) man was starting to make pottery and farm the land. These Neolithic ancestors left behind a number of burial mounds, such as the one at Whiteleaf Hill (Walk 13).

This was also the time of the Icknield Way – a prehistoric 'highway' that allowed people to move through the heavily wooded countryside on a route stretching from Dorset and Wiltshire to Norfolk. These ancient trackways were later used by invading Saxons and Vikings, and later still by drovers driving animals to market. Even today, the Ridgeway National Trail follows their route.

The discovery of bronze and, later, iron allowed agriculture to develop further. Our Iron Age ancestors also built a number of forts to help defend their land, and the earthworks of these can still be seen today, such as at Cholesbury (Walk 10). Recent evidence now suggests that Grim's Ditch – the name given to several linear earthworks that can be found in the Chilterns, including Hastoe, Pitstone Hill, and Nuffield – dates back to the Iron Age.

The Iron Age was brought to a close by a full-scale Roman invasion in AD43 – although their impact on the Chilterns was limited to the building of villas (including those along the Hambelden, Chess and Gade river valleys) and the formation of a network of roads, including some that are still used today.

Following the Battle of Hastings in 1066, Anglo-Saxon landowners were replaced by those loyal to William the Conqueror. Manors were formed that later morphed into the country estates still in evidence today. The Normans also built motte and bailey castles, such as at Berkhamsted (Walk 9), and many of the area's churches originate from this period, albeit having undergone a fair number of alterations over the centuries. This was also a time of great monasteries and abbeys such as Ashridge (Walk 9) and Missenden (Walk 17).

The Chilterns are a mainly agricultural region, although over the centuries the area has seen various cottage industries come and go, from straw-platting to lace-making, as well as small-scale brick- and tile-making. The abundant supply of wood helped the furniture industry to flourish and

The view over Princes Risborough from Whiteleaf Hill above the Whiteleaf Cross (Walk 13)

The 16th-century dovecote at Monks Risborough (just off Walk 13)

there were at one time many local bodgers making chair legs and spindles, using nothing more sophisticated than a simple pole lathe and a chisel.

More recently the increase in transport links, including a number of railways, and – especially during the latter half of the 20th century – the rise in car-ownership, has meant that the Chilterns has come within commuting distance of London. However, all is not lost: much of the Chilterns has been designated an Area of Outstanding Natural Beauty, and this, along with the tremendous efforts of the Chiltern Society, should help to preserve this special area for future generations.

WHERE TO STAY

The Chilterns region has a wide range of accommodation, ranging from youth hostels and campsites to pubs with rooms, guesthouses and hotels. To find out more about accommodation, visit the tourist information websites listed in Appendix B.

GETTING TO AND AROUND THE CHILTERNS

Major roads passing through the Chilterns include the M40, M1, A413, A41 and A5. If travelling by car to any of the walks, always remember to park considerately and never block access routes.

Rail services and stations that give access to the Chilterns AONB, include:

- Goring-on-Thames: trains between London, West of England, South Wales and the Midlands
- Henley-on-Thames: branch line from Twyford (connections to London, West of England and South Wales)
- High Wycombe and Princes Risborough: trains between London and the Midlands
- Little Chalfont, Amersham, Great Missenden and Wendover: trains between London and Aylesbury
- Berkhamsted and Tring: trains between London and the Midlands
- Luton: trains between London, the North, Gatwick and Brighton
- Hitchin: trains between London and the North

Where specific walks can be accessed by train, the nearest station is listed in the relevant information box. Some of the walks may also be accessed using buses and brief information is also provided for this; however, for the latest information relating to public transport use the contact details listed in Appendix B.

FOOD AND DRINK

Some of the walks start at places where food and drink may be bought, whether at a shop, café or pub; some offer opportunities for stopping off

The timber-framed Bull and Butcher pub at Turville (Walk 23)

en route at a pub or shop – although these are not always conveniently placed around the route. Brief details of refreshment opportunities are given in the information box at the start of each route, but bear in mind that there is no guarantee they'll be open when required. Therefore it's always a good idea to carry some food and drink with you, along with a small 'emergency ration' in case of an unexpected delay.

WALKING IN THE CHILTERNS

The walks in this guide range from 7.2km to 18.8km (4½ miles to 11¾ miles) and cover fairly low-level terrain (below 267m), and although some have several, sometimes steep,

climbs and descents, they should be suitable for most walkers. The routes follow well-defined tracks and paths, although some follow narrow and at times indistinct paths, especially through woods, where careful navigation may be required.

Make every effort to avoid disturbing the wildlife and keep dogs under close control at all times.

As for the weather, summers tend to be fairly dry and warm; this is also the time of year with the highest number of visitors. Spring and autumn offer some of the best walking conditions: spring heralds new life in the Chilterns, with vivid greens on the trees, colourful displays of flowers and abundant birdsong, while cool autumn nights herald a dramatic

Autumn colours at Stonor Park (Walk 24)

change, with the leaves on the trees turning spectacular shades of russet, gold and brown. During the winter months, spells of rain can make some routes quite muddy. However, walking on a clear, frosty winter's day can be a magical experience.

Always choose clothing suitable for the season, along with a waterproof jacket, comfortable and waterproof footwear and a comfortable rucksack. On wet days gaiters or waterproof trousers can be very useful. It's also worth carrying a basic first aid kit in case of minor accidents.

Long-distance routes

If you fancy a much longer walk you could give either the Chiltern Way or the Ridgeway a try.

The Chiltern Way – a 214km (134-mile) route that can be extended to include the new Berkshire Loop and other Chilterns highlights – weaves its way around all corners of the Chiltern AONB, while the northern section of the Ridgeway National Trail runs for 71km (44 miles) along the length of the Chilterns from the River Thames at Goring to Ivinghoe Beacon.

Some other long-distance routes that pass through parts of the Chilterns include:

- Aylesbury Ring and Outer Ring: two circular routes of 50km (31 miles) or 85km (53 miles) skirting around Aylesbury
- Chess Valley Way: 17km (10½-mile) route alongside the River Chess between Chesham and Rickmansworth
- Hertfordshire Way: 267km (166-mile) circular route meandering around the county
- North Bucks Way: 53km (33-mile) linear route from the Ridgeway at Chequers to Pulpit Hill, meandering through North Buckinghamshire
- Oxfordshire Way: 105km (65-mile) linear route from Bourton-on-the-Water through the Cotswolds and Chilterns AONB to the River Thames at Henley-on-Thames
- South Bucks Way: 37km (23-mile) linear route from Coombe Hill near Wendover to the Grand Union Canal at Denham
- Swan's Way: 105km (65-mile) linear route from Salcey Forest in Northamptonshire through Buckinghamshire to Goring-on-Thames in Oxfordshire.

MAPS

The Ordnance Survey (OS) offer two series of maps: the 1:50,000 (2cm to 1km) Landranger series and the more detailed 1:25,000 (4cm to 1km) Explorer series. The OS maps covering the Chilterns AONB are:

- Landranger: 165, 166, 174 (for very small parts of walks 27 and 34) and 175
- Explorer: 171, 172, 181, 182, and 193

This guide features extracts of the OS 1:50,000 Landranger series, , increased to 1:40,000 for greater clarity, but it is advisable to always carry the relevant Explorer map with you when walking.

WAYMARKING, ACCESS AND RIGHTS OF WAY

The rights of way throughout the Chilterns are typically well signposted with a mix of fingerposts, marker posts and waymarks on fences and

Typical waymarks

gateposts. The descriptions in this guide, in combination with the map extracts and good signage on the ground, should make route-finding straightforward; however, it is still advisable to carry a compass and the relevant OS Explorer map.

The walks in this guide follow official rights of way, whether they be footpaths, bridleways, restricted byways or byways. Some routes also pass through areas of open access land (marked on OS Explorer maps) where you can freely roam.

Rights of way are:
- Footpaths – yellow arrow – walkers only
- Bridleways – blue arrow – walkers, cyclists and horse riders
- Restricted byways – purple arrow – walkers, cyclists, horse riders and carriage drivers
- Byways – red arrow – same as for restricted byways, plus motorcycles and motorised vehicles

The Countryside Code
When out walking, please respect the countryside and follow the Countryside Code:
- Be safe – plan ahead and follow any signs
- Leave gates and property as you find them
- Protect plants and animals, and take your litter home
- Keep dogs under close control
- Consider other people
  Finally, always take care when either walking on or crossing roads.

Following field boundaries up to Ewelme Park (Walk 26)

USING THIS GUIDE

The descriptions in this guidebook all follow the same format. The information box gives the start/finish location, accompanied by a grid reference and any parking details (alternative start points are included, where possible, to facilitate approach by both train and car); walk distance (kilometres/ miles); ascent (metres); minimum time (hours); relevant map details; places that offer refreshments (pubs, cafés and shops); and brief public transport information.

This is followed by a short introduction to the route, identifying any major points of interest, including villages. The route is then described in detail, with various, easily identifiable items or places of interest highlighted in bold type. Background information is also given for places of interest.

The route summary table in Appendix A provides the key statistics for all of the walks, and Appendix B contains contact details that may be helpful in planning a visit to the Chilterns.

Times and distances

The distances quoted for each walk – metric first, with approximate imperial conversions rounded to the nearest $1/4$, $1/2$, $3/4$ or whole number – have been measured from OS Explorer maps; note that the heights quoted on the maps are in metres and the grid lines are spaced at intervals of 1km. The walking time for each walk has been worked out using a walking

The view looking west on the way between Turville Heath and Pishill (Walk 24) – allow time to take a seat and admire the view

speed of 4km/hour (2½ miles/hour) plus 10 minutes for every 100m of ascent. This should be treated as the **minimum** amount of walking time required to undertake the walk. It does not include any time for rests, photography, consulting the map or guidebook, or simply admiring the view – all of which can add substantially to the day's activity.

Maps

The map extracts are from the 1:50,000 OS Landranger series, increased to 1:40,000 for greater clarity. Features showing on the map that are mentioned in the route are highlighted in bold text to help you follow the route.

Longer walks

Some of the walks in this guide could be easily combined (although directions for this are not given). These routes are:

- Shared (no extension required): 5 and 6; 6 and 7; 11 and 12; 24 and 25; 28 and 33; 31 and 32
- Short extension required: 2 and 3; 12 and 13; 13 and 14; 15 and 16; 23 and 24; 24 and 32; 25 and 26; 25 and 29; 27 and 28; 27 and 29; 28 and 29

1 NORTH OF LUTON

The route heads along the edge of the trees that crown the Sharpenhoe Clappers (Walk 1)

WALK 1
Harlington and Sharpenhoe Clappers

Start/finish	Village hall car park on Sundon Road in Harlington (TL 037 304), 2km east from M1 Junction 12; or Harlington railway station (TL 034 304). Car drivers may also start at Sharpenhoe Clappers car park (TL 065 295)
Distance	9.2km (5¾ miles)
Ascent	175m
Time	2½hrs
Map	OS Explorer 193
Refreshments	Shop, Carpenters Arms (01525 872384) and The Old Sun (01525 877330) at Harlington
Public transport	Bus and train links to Harlington

This walk, the first of three exploring the outlying section of the Chilterns AONB to the north of Luton, sets out from Harlington, where the preacher John Bunyan was arrested, and heads south-east up to the tree-crowned Sharpenhoe Clappers for some lovely views. The route then drops steeply down to Sharpenhoe before meandering back through fields to Harlington.

To start from the railway station turn right over the bridge, follow Station Road up to the crossroads and turn right on Sundon Road.

From the village hall in Harlington, with the Carpenters Arms opposite, cross over Sundon Road, turn left and go downhill for 250m, soon passing The Old Sun. ◀ Continue past Kent Court (left), and just after a row of white cottages (also left) turn left across the road and follow the narrow signed path beside the driveway, passing a house. Keep ahead to a field. Head diagonally right with a distant view of Sharpenhoe Clappers. At the far side bear right along the field margin through two fields and continue straight on across the middle of the next field. Pass through the boundary and bear left (east) along the left-hand field margin. Cross a footbridge and turn right along the minor road for 400m, then turn left past a gate, following the track for 450m.

HARLINGTON

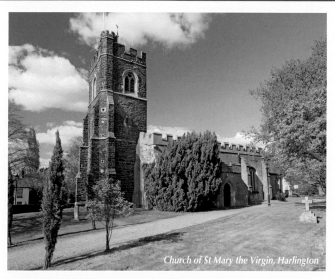

Church of St Mary the Virgin, Harlington

At the time of the Domesday Book, Harlington was known as Herlingdone and the lord of the manor was Nigel D'Albini. Several hundred years later the 17th-century non-conformist preacher John Bunyan (1628–1688) was arrested here for holding an unauthorised religious gathering. It was during his imprisonment at Bedford gaol that he wrote *The Pilgrim's Progress*, and many believe the Sharpenhoe Clappers along with the Barton Hills (Walk 2) and Pegsdon Hills (Walk 3) gave him the inspiration for his 'Delectable Mountains'. Visit the 700-year-old Church of St Mary the Virgin to see a stained glass window commemorating Bunyan.

It was from the village green that the first English National Steeplechase (flat horse race over fences) took place in 1830 on a 4¼-mile course to the obelisk at Wrest Park, Silsoe (the obelisk was moved to Trent Park in 1934).

At the trees (surrounding a hidden pond), where the field narrows turn right through the hedge and continue east-south-east (diagonally left) up across the field. Go through a gate and head south-south-east up through the

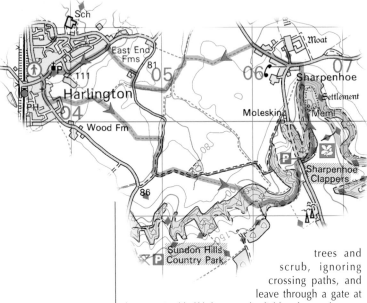

trees and scrub, ignoring crossing paths, and leave through a gate at the top. Head half-left across the field and enter the trees where the path splits. Follow the right-hand path (Chiltern Way and John Bunyan Trail) heading east to a path junction; keep ahead (left-hand fork), with a fence to the right and trees on the left, to reach another junction. Keep left through the gate and head slightly right (north) across the field, then go through a gate in the hedge on the right and cross the road to Sharpenhoe clappers **car park**.

Follow the surfaced path for 200m, then fork left along the Chiltern Way and The Bunyan Trail, heading among trees, to reach a grassy area. Keep to the path along the lower-left edge; it soon meanders through the trees of **Sharpenhoe Clappers**.

Sharpenhoe Clappers is crowned both by the remains of an Iron Age promontory hill fort and a lovely beech wood. Hidden among the trees is the Robertson Memorial, commemorating two brothers who died in action during WWI. The site was also used as a medieval rabbit warren; 'Clappers' is thought to derive from the French *clapier* or the medieval Latin term *claperius*, meaning a rabbit warren or pile of stones.

At the northern end follow a path steeply down steps towards Sharpenhoe, keep ahead and continue down the left-hand field margin to a road just south of a former **moated manor**.

A former owner of Sharpenhoe's **moated manor** was Thomas Norton (1532–1584), who, along with Thomas Sackville, wrote the play *Gorboduc* – claimed to be the earliest English tragedy.

Turn left, keep ahead at the junction, continue to the end of the village and turn left past a gate (footpath sign) to follow the right-hand field margin. In the next field bear right to follow the right-hand boundary along two sides of the field, 300m along the second side turn right

Looking north-west out over the village of Sharpenhoe from Sharpenhoe Clappers

From Sharpenhoe the walk heads through fields back towards Harlington

over a footbridge and then go left. Follow the left-hand field margin to a minor road and turn right for 150m. At the buildings on the left (Willow Farm) go left along the driveway and soon keep ahead on a path (just right of the driveway) heading up to Barton Road in **Harlington**.

Cross over and turn left (to your left are views of the Sinodun Hills and Sharpenhoe Clappers); at the right-hand bend cross over again and follow the surfaced path straight on, heading west across the park with the pond (often dry) and then the **church** on your right. Leave through the gate and continue along Church Road to a crossroads beside the war memorial (left) and village sign (right); go left (Sundon Road) for the village hall or straight on (Station Road) for the railway station.

WALK 2

Barton-le-Clay, Hexton and the Barton Hills

Start/finish	Church Road in Barton-le-Clay (TL 085 304), accessed from the A6; limited roadside parking
Distance	15.7km (9¾ miles) or 10.9km (6¾ miles)
Ascent	250m or 170m
Time	4½hrs or 3hrs
Map	OS Explorer 193
Refreshments	The Raven (01582 881209) and Lavender Tea Room (07805 815672) at Hexton; Lilley Arms (01462 768371) at Lilley
Public transport	Bus links to Barton-Le-Clay from Bedford and Luton

From Barton-le-Clay the walk heads east below the Chiltern escarpment to the neighbouring village of Hexton. From here the route climbs up onto the chalk hills, taking in parts of the Icknield Way, Chiltern Way and John Bunyan Trail, to pass through peaceful Lilley before heading northwards to the Barton Hills. A final descent through the nature reserve with some great views leads back to Barton-le-Clay. A shorter walk, missing out Lilley, is also described.

From the church in Barton-le-Clay head north along Church Road, cross over Hexton Road (B655), turn right and then left along Manor Road and continue for 500m, passing a school.

St Nicholas' Church

Barton-le-Clay, overlooked by the Barton Hills that form the northern extremity of the Chiltern Hills AONB, is home to the 800-year-old **St Nicholas' Church**, whose Perpendicular-styled chequer-patterned tower was added in the 15th century.

Some 100m after the school, turn right on a surfaced path and soon go over a footbridge;

bear left alongside the field edge and then go right, following the field edge and the John Bunyan Trail.

Continue eastwards for 800m; at the end of a section of hedge turn left for 75m and then right to follow a hedge on the right, still heading eastwards, through two fields. Cross a footbridge at the corner, with trees to the right, and head half-right across the field towards houses near **Manor Farm**. Turn right along the road to reach a T-junction and go right through **Hexton**, soon passing The Raven on the right and the village hall (left), which is home to the Lavender Tea Room.

Colourful pub sign in Hexton

> The small village of **Hexton** lies along a single main street with the mid 18th-century Hexton Manor hidden off to the east. To the south-west of the village centre is St Faith's Church, which underwent Victorian restorations and has recently been refurbished as both a church and community centre. Further to the south-south-west are the heavily wooded remains of Ravensburgh Castle – a former Iron Age hill fort dating from 400BC (no public access).

At the crossroads, beside the 19th-century water pump, go straight over the B655 and follow the Lilley road for 175m. (To visit the church go right along the B655 for 200m.) Fork right along a track for 350m, and where the track turns right go straight on up between the trees on **Gravel Hill**. Keep ahead through the field, following the right-hand boundary. Go through into the next field and turn right, then go left at the corner (staying in the same field) to follow the hedge on the right (south) to a minor road.

Shortcut

Turn right along the road, continue for 150m and then turn left, following the surfaced drive (bridleway) past **Mortgrove Farm**. Then follow the fence and hedge under the power lines to a track; turn right following the Icknield Way and Chiltern Way to a cross-track junction (TL 096 274) and turn right again to rejoin the main walk.

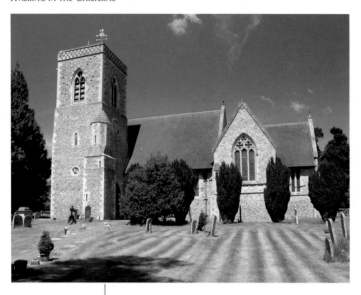

St Peter's Church at Lilley

Turn left to a T-junction and then right to a right-hand bend. Go left, following the byway through the trees for 50m, and then turn right on a track (bridleway and John Bunyan Trail), along the right-hand field edge for 700m, soon passing power lines. Keep to the track as it goes left and right, and where it goes left again (permissive path) go straight on along the field edge through two fields, keeping ahead at a cross junction to reach the far corner. Go left for 75m and then right through a gate and follow the hedge on the right through two fields to a crossing bridleway. Turn right to **Lilley** and go left along the road.

Lilley is home to a pub and a church, St Peter's, that dates back to the 12th century (although it was rebuilt in the 19th century). Inside the church there are some original features, colourful stained glass windows and a fine Elizabethan heraldic memorial to Thomas Docwra, Prior of the Order of St John of Jerusalem (1458–1527).

At the small village green, with the **church** ahead, turn sharp right along West Street and continue past The Lilley Arms. After the last house keep ahead along the track, later passing **Ward's Wood**. Keep ahead at a crossing bridleway for 150m and at the next junction fork right (straight on) to a cross-track junction (TL 096 274 – the point at which the shortcut rejoins the main route). Continue straight on (John Bunyan Trail and Chiltern Way), following the right-hand hedge through two fields and passing the power lines to reach a road with **Barton Hill Farm** to the right.

Cross over and turn left along the road for 125m, then turn right past a vehicle barrier, following the track (Chiltern Way) northwards with the hedge on your right and later continuing straight on between fields to the northern boundary. Keep ahead into the next field following the right-hand hedge for 25m and then turn right through a gate. Fork right at the split and shortly go through a gate, continue to reach a seat with lovely views across the **Barton Hills**.

After Lilley the route meanders past Ward's Wood following good tracks

Looking north over the Barton Hills nature reserve

Barton Hills National Nature Reserve has a mix of flower-rich chalk grassland with plants including fleawort, greater pignut and pasqueflower, along with areas of woodland and a variety of butterflies during the summer. The information board features a map showing a number of paths that meander through the reserve if you want to explore.

Continue along the upper edge and turn left at the corner, staying inside the reserve, and follow the fence on the right for 900m, later heading downhill with views ahead towards Barton-le-Clay. Go through a gate on the right and continue downhill, passing a section of steps, before bearing left to another gate. Enter the field and follow the right-hand field edge, soon curving left (west). Continue along the track and turn right along the lane to the church at **Barton-le-Clay**.

WALK 3
Pirton and the Pegsdon Hills

Start/finish	Great Green in Pirton, opposite the Motte and Bailey pub (TL 145 315)
Distance	10.9km (6¾ miles)
Ascent	240m
Time	3¼hrs
Map	OS Explorer 193
Refreshments	Shops, Motte and Bailey pub (01462 712730) and The Fox (01462 712691) at Pirton; Live and Let Live (01582 881739) at Pegsdon.
Public transport	Bus links from Hitchin to Pirton (excluding Sundays)

From Great Green, which was once known as Chipping Green ('chipping' is derived from the Anglo-Saxon word for market, so this may have been the site of a local market), the route passes the earthworks of a former medieval castle before heading up onto the chalk downs. After crossing Telegraph Hill the walk visits the convoluted chalk grassland of the Pegsdon Hills Nature Reserve before dropping down to Pegsdon, following the Chiltern Way. The final stretch heads past Knocking Hoe National Nature Reserve and back to Pirton.

St Mary's Church, Pirton

35

PIRTON

The Fox – one of two pubs in Pirton

The village of Pirton, which lies just to the north of the convoluted chalk hills, is centred on Toot Hill (meaning 'lookout'). The 'hill' is actually part of a medieval motte and bailey castle that was built by the de Limesy family, one-time lords of the manor. Besides the hill, or motte, there were two outer defensive areas (baileys); the 11th-century Parish Church of St Mary lies within the eastern bailey and the grassy area to the south of the castle and church, known as 'The Bury', was once the site of the ancient village that was abandoned in the 19th century. The east-west linear depression that can be seen was once a street known as Lad's Orchard Lane, while the raised areas were where the houses stood.

From the village green in Pirton, stand facing the Motte and Bailey pub and head north-east along Crabtree Lane (just left of the pub) for 75m. Shortly before Docklands Road (left) turn right on a surfaced path (Icknield Way). (At the end of Crabtree Lane is the High Street with The Fox opposite and the village shop to the right.) The path soon bends left to reach two gates with the former castle motte (small hill) on the right. The first gate leads into St Mary's churchyard; however, we go through the other gate into the field and bear right, with a fence on the right, before continuing southwards across the field known as 'The Bury' (the right of way heads south-east to the boundary and then turns right).

Go through the gate in the southern corner of the field, turn right (Walnut Tree Road) to a road junction (Hitchin Road), cross over and go straight on (south-west) along the bridleway with the hedge on your right for 500m. Turn left along the track, following the right-hand field boundary, and where the track turns left, fork right through a gate, following the left-hand boundary uphill with a

37

Heading north through the Pegsdon Hills Nature Reserve

The late 16th-century house was built for Thomas Docwra, Prior of the Order of St John of Jerusalem (1458–1527).

farm building and then High Down House over to the left. ◄

Where the boundary curves left keep straight on (south-west) across the field and go through a gate near the corner. Keep ahead (south) into a field and follow the right-hand boundary downhill (Chiltern way). Bear left on a path through the trees and turn right across the road. Keep ahead through the open field to pass just right of a tree-shaded pit; ignore a crossing path and go through a gate in the field corner near **Old Wellbury**.

Follow the right-hand boundary hedge as it curves left and right, soon descending between hedges. Keep ahead between buildings at **New Wellbury**; bear slightly left and go through a gate on the right-hand side of the track. Continue through the trees, turn left on the sur-faced track to reach a junction and go right.

Keep to the track as it passes between **Wellbury House** (hidden in the trees on the left) and a house on the right; go into an open field and soon turn right (Chiltern Way) heading south-west across the field. Pass just right of the trees and keep ahead uphill, going straight on towards **Little Offley**, then follow the track between farm buildings and past a lovely brick-faced house that dates from Tudor times. Keep to the track as it soon bears right and then turn left into a field. Follow the left-hand field boundary and keep ahead through the trees at **Lilley Hoo**. Continue across the field to the track and hedge, turn right for 50m to a split and go straight on (right-hand fork) across the field with **Telegraph Hill** on your left. Continue through the trees to join the Icknield Way.

Turn right for 50m and then go left through a gate to enter the nature reserve on Pegsdon Hills.

Owned by the Hertfordshire and Middlesex Wildlife Trust, the steeply folded contours of the Pegsdon Hills **Nature Reserve** are home to a mix of flower-rich chalk grassland and woodland. The information board shows a variety of paths that can be followed through the reserve.

Keep ahead (north-west), soon following a fence on the right. (A gate on the right gives access to a seat with a great view.) ▶ Continue alongside the fence, then go through a gate and head downhill past a seat with a deep coombe, or dry valley, to your right. Keep ahead through gates, heading north towards **Pegsdon**. Leave the nature reserve, cross the road (B655) and take the lane opposite. Bear left at the junction for 120m and then right along Pegsdon Way, with houses on your right, later passing the Live and Let Live pub.

The walk now follows the Chiltern Way back to Pirton.

Turn left at the junction (Chiltern Way) and follow the surfaced track for 500m. Shortly after the left-hand bend, turn right and go across the field and uphill, with trees on your left and a shallow valley to the right. Follow the field edge for 120m and then turn left, continuing in the same field (with the boundary on your right) to the far side. Turn right and go uphill, following the fence (left) to a junction with a bridleway at the top. Take a seat and admire the views to the north (the gate gives access to Knocking Hoe National Nature Reserve – home to chalk

Enjoy the view north across the Knocking Hoe National Nature Reserve before descending back to Pirton

grassland plants including the nationally rare burnt-tip orchid). Turn left for 100m and then left again at the next junction, heading down Wood Lane (track) for 1.4km to **Pirton**. Cross the road and take the road opposite (Great Green) back to the village green.

2 DUNSTABLE TO BERKHAMSTED

Heading east along the ridge towards Gallows Hill (Walk 5)

WALK 4
Whipsnade, Studham and the Dunstable Downs

Start/finish	Tree Cathedral car park, Whipsnade (TL 009 180)
Alternative starts	Studham Common car park (TL 023 157); Chiltern Gateway Centre car park (TL 008 194)
Distance	16.1km (10 miles) – southern loop 8km (5 miles); northern loop 8km (5 miles)
Ascent	325m – southern loop 130m; northern loop 195m
Time	5hrs – southern loop 2½hrs; northern loop 2½hrs
Maps	OS Explorer 181, 182 and 193
Refreshments	The Bell (01582 872460) and Red Lion (01582 872530) at Studham; café at Chiltern Gateway Centre (01582 500920)
Public transport	Bus links (excluding Sunday) to Whipsnade, Chiltern Gateway Centre and Studham from Dunstable, St Albans and Hemel Hempstead

A figure-of-eight walk that can be split into two shorter 8km (5-mile) walks, taking in some great views from the Dunstable Downs and visiting historic churches in Whipsnade and Studham. While passing the perimeter fence of Whipsnade Zoo on the southern loop you might catch sight of some of the animals.

Southern Loop

From the car park head back along the entrance track and fork left along Bushey Close, cross the road and bear half-left across the grass towards the church.

The **Church of St Mary Magdalene** in Whipsnade dates from the late 16th century, with the tower being the oldest part. Step inside to the see the 17th-century (Jacobean) carved wood pulpit with tester, as well as a painting of the Royal Arms of George I, which has been painted over those of Queen Anne and James I.

Go through the churchyard, keeping right of the church, and leave through a gate. Once in the field, follow the left-hand hedge and continue through the next field – but now with the hedge on your right – to a gate. Cross the road, turn left for 50m and then turn right into a field, following the edge of Heath Wood (left) to the field corner. Continue along the enclosed path between houses to an estate road; turn left for 130m, and after the seventh driveway on the left turn left again along the enclosed path. Soon, follow the path as it swings right and runs parallel to the lane (left) with gardens and houses to the right. At a junction, at the end of the houses, turn right up the path (not the permissive bridle-way) and soon enter a field. Keep ahead alongside the right-hand boundary, pass a wood and then bear slightly left across the field towards some trees. Keep ahead, staying close to the right-hand edge of the wood, descending to a road.

Turn left along Dunstable Road for 75m, and then go right across the road and through a gate. Continue up the right-hand field margin for 200m to a path junction and turn left, staying in the same field (hedge on right), following two sides of the field. Just before the next hedge corner, turn right through the hedge and go alongside the fence, soon with houses on the right, to a road in **Studham** – Bedfordshire's southernmost village – with The Bell pub opposite (said to be county's highest pub).

War Memorial at Studham

43

Turn right and at the crossroads, beside the unusual War Memorial, go right along Church Road.

Just past The Red Lion, cross the road to a fingerpost and follow the bridleway (not the path) heading south-west across the common for 250m. Pass left of the Old School House and follow the field margin past a school. Cross the road and follow the right-hand field margin; keep ahead into the next field for 75m and turn right over a stile, heading north-east across the field. At the far side bear left alongside the trees and go through a gate. Go right along the track and then left along the lane towards the church, passing **Manor Farm**.

Go through the churchyard, passing left of the 13th-century Church of St Mary the Virgin, and leave through the gate. ◄ Turn left, cross the track and continue westwards through the gate to follow the right-hand field edge. Go through a gate, cross the footbridge and turn right along the **Chiltern Way** (which is followed back towards Whipsnade). Leave the trees and follow the farm track along the right-hand edge of two fields. Once in the trees, keep ahead (right) at a junction and follow the boundary fence of **Whipsnade Zoo** on the left.

> The early 13th century church houses an interesting Norman font decorated with dragons.

Whipsnade Zoo, owned by the Zoological Society of London – a charity devoted to the conservation of animals and their habitats – has around 3000 animals, a café and a narrow gauge steam railway (01582 872171).

Turn left along surfaced track (Studham Lane) and at the road take the right-hand fork for 150m towards **Whipsnade**. Bear half right up across the common, cross the road and follow the track back to the car park.

Northern Loop

From the back of the car park go through the gate towards the **Tree Cathedral** – which was created by Edmund Kell Blyth in the 1930s and is now managed by the National Trust – and bear left alongside the trees (Icknield Way) to a gate.

Heading north below the Dunstable Downs – north loop

Keep ahead, following the left-hand fence, then go through a gate and turn right along the track (Icknield Way) for 600m to reach an open grassy area near Bison Hill car park with a good view to the west.

To the right is the Icknield Way and straight on is the car park: go half-right (north-west) between these two for 150m, ignoring two crossing routes, and then follow the bridleway steeply downhill, staying parallel with the road. At the second gate on the right, just before a T-junction with a bridleway, turn right through the gate and follow a path along the lower edge of the **Dunstable Downs** for 300m, with a bridleway running parallel on the left.

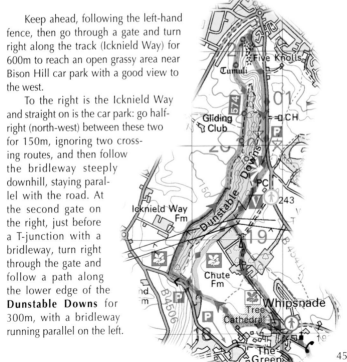

Go through another gate and continue along the bridle-way. Shortly after the overhead power lines go through a gate to follow another parallel path for 700m. Go through a gate and continue straight on for 75m. Keep left at a split and follow the path along the lower edge of the scarp with the **gliding club** to the left for 1.6km, ignoring all paths off to the right.

On reaching an open grassy area between trees on the edge of **Dunstable**, turn right and right again up to a gate and follow the path southwards past **Five Knolls** (a group of 4000-year-old Late Neolithic or Early Bronze Age burial mounds) to the summit above Pascomb Pit.

There are some great **views** from here: to the north-east is Dunstable and Luton, and to the north-west is Totternhoe (close by) with Leighton Buzzard beyond. Quainton Hill is 25km away to the west, while much nearer and west-south-west is Edlesborough church. Ivinghoe Beacon is to the south-west and the Dunstable Downs are directly southwards.

The Windcatcher – an eco-friendly ventilation system for the visitor centre – north loop

Bear left (clockwise) around the top of Pascomb Pit to reach a surfaced path. ▸ Head south along the surfaced path – or after 400m fork right and follow the parallel grassy path close to the right-hand fence – to reach the Windcatcher, 75m to the right of the Chiltern Gateway Centre.

> This exposed hilltop location has been used for two **signalling systems**, although nothing remains today. The first used fires to send signals when England was threatened by the Spanish Armada, and a later one, using a shutter system, formed part of a line between London and Great Yarmouth, built in response to the threat of a French invasion.

Keep ahead, soon staying on the right-hand side of the hedge, then go through a gate and continue for 200m, passing under the power lines to a junction at the corner of the trees. Turn left (Chiltern Way), go through a gate and continue alongside Chute Wood. Keep ahead across the surfaced track and at the split, beside a communications mast, fork right (Chiltern Way), soon passing **Chute Farm**. Follow the surfaced drive past Sallowsprings (houses) and at the end of the left-hand fence go left into Sallowsprings Nature Reserve. Follow the left-hand edge, turn right at the corner still following the left-hand edge through the reserve. Rejoin the drive for 100m; turn right for 25m – ahead is an entrance to the Tree Cathedral – and turn left between hedges to go back to the car park at **Whipsnade**.

This deep coombe was at one time used for orange-rolling on Good Friday, with participants chasing oranges down the steep slope.

WALK 5

Ivinghoe Beacon, Ivinghoe and Pitstone

Start/finish	Pitstone Hill car park (SP 954 149), 700m off the B488 to the south-east of Ivinghoe
Distance	13km (8 miles) or 8.4km (5¼ miles)
Ascent	300m or 215m
Time	3¾hrs or 2½hrs
Map	OS Explorer 181
Refreshments	Rose and Crown (01296 668472) at Ivinghoe
Public transport	Bus links to Ivinghoe from Aylesbury, Dunstable and Leighton Buzzard

This walk follows the Ridgeway up past Incombe Hole to Ivinghoe Beacon – a great viewpoint – before heading east to Gallows Hill with views of the Dunstable Downs. It then meanders through woods and open countryside to arrive back at Incombe Hole, where there is the option of cutting the walk short and returning to the start point. The longer walk heads down through Ivinghoe and Pitstone, passing a windmill before climbing back up to the car park.

From the car park cross the minor road, go through the gate and follow the Ridgeway with views of Steps Hill ahead. At the cross-junction go straight on up beside the deep hollow, or coombe, of Incombe Hole (a sign indicates that this area was once used for military training – so do not touch any unidentified objects). Near the top, **don't go through the gate** but keep left of the fence and head over **Steps Hill**, looking out for the marker post. Follow the path through the bushes and then alongside the fence and through a gate.

Continue along the path, soon dropping down to a minor road. Cross over and keep ahead, following the Ridgeway up the broad ridge to the trig point (230m) on Ivinghoe Beacon – marked on the map as **Beacon Hill** – and a great panoramic view.

Following the Ridgeway towards the Ivinghoe Hills

Beacon Hill, a favoured location for model
plane flyers, was the site of an Iron Age
hill fort, although little of it remains
today. To the south-west, views
stretch back along the
Chiltern scarp,

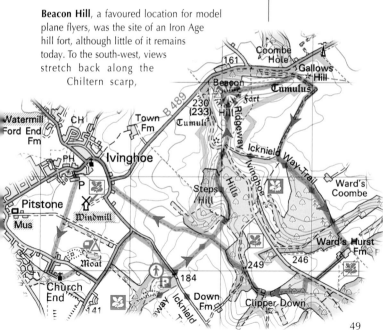

49

and further to the right are the Tring Reservoirs. Continue across the flat expanse of the Vale of Aylesbury and to the north is Leighton Buzzard, with Milton Keynes beyond. To the north-east is the nearby church at Edlesborough, while to the east are views along the broad ridge past Gallows Hill to the white chalk figure of the Whipsnade Lion, on the side of the Dunstable Downs, completed in 1933.

Turn right and head east along the broad ridge towards **Gallows Hill** for 900m, passing through two gates to a path junction (SP 968 170), some 125m beyond the second gate. Turn right down to the trees and go right again (trees on left), keep ahead across the field, then alongside more trees and then through a gate. Turn left for 175m, following the trees, and go through another gate. Continue south-eastwards, following the Icknield Way through the trees and keeping ahead at a crossing track. Head steeply up steps beside a fence, go through a gate and follow the fence on the right. Go through another gate and turn right between the buildings of **Ward's Hurst Farm**. Head south-west along the concrete track.

Cross the minor road and bear right along the path just inside the wood, later bearing left onto a wide track. Turn right and follow the track for 700m, passing **Clipper Down** (Walk 6 heads along here in the opposite direction). Fork left down a waymarked path, go through a gate and continue in the same direction, downhill, to a fence. Keep ahead, following the fence on the left to a cross-junction that you passed earlier. ◄

To cut the walk short, turn left here and go back to the car park.

Keep straight on, passing some hawthorn bushes; go through a gate and keep ahead, passing the end of a fence/hedge, head north-west across the field, later following the right-hand field edge to the corner. Dogleg right through the gate and follow the enclosed path to reach a road (B488).

Turn right towards **Ivinghoe**, keeping ahead at the junction and later passing the church (100m along

Vicarage Lane on the right is the Rose and Crown pub) to reach a junction beside the village green. ▸

> The cruciform-shaped **Church of St Mary the Virgin**, which dates from the early 13th century, dominates the centre of Ivinghoe. Inside there are some interesting 15th-century bench ends (or poppy-heads); a Jacobean pulpit and large carved wooden angels in the roof.

Continue along the High Street (B489) for 175m, and as the road bends right, after passing Groomsby Drive, turn left along Green Lane between houses. The track soon becomes a path passing Orchard House, keep ahead through a gate. Head south-south-west across the field, with the **windmill** to your left, to reach a crossing track. (To visit the windmill – National Trust: 01442 851227 – detour left and left again (permissive path); for the Pitstone Green Museum of Rural Life – 01582 605464 or 792701 – take the track to the right.)

Some 600m to the right along Station Road is Ford End Watermill, which dates back to 1616 and is the only remaining working watermill in Buckinghamshire.

The early 17th-century Pitstone Windmill

Pitstone **windmill** dates from 1627 and is possibly the oldest post mill in England. This type of mill is such that the complete windmill rotates on the post to align its sails to the wind.

Continue straight on, pass through a line of bushes and follow the grass strip between fields towards **Pitstone**. Go through a gate and turn left along the road, and after 50m turn right along Church Road, following it as it bends left to a **church**.

The redundant 13th-century **St Mary's Church** in Pitstone (cared for by the Churches Conservation Trust) was at one time connected with the priory at Ashridge. Inside there is a carved Norman font, a 14th-century brass, interesting woodwork and 18th-century wall paintings.

At the churchyard gate, turn left through a hedge-gap into the field and follow the path around two sides of the churchyard wall on the right, then turn left, following the right-hand field boundary. Go through a gate and turn right up Vicarage Road; cross over the B488 and turn left, following the path parallel to the road for 650m. Keep to the path as it curves right and heads uphill parallel with the minor road. Go through a gate and keep ahead (open access land) for 175m before bearing left to the car park.

WALK 6
Grand Union Canal, Pitstone Hill and Aldbury

Start/finish	Tring Station (SP 950 122) to the west of Tring; roadside parking along Beggars Lane. Car drivers could also start at Pitstone Hill car park (SP 954 149)
Distance	11.9km (7½ miles)
Ascent	305m
Time	3½hrs
Map	OS Explorer 181
Refreshments	Brownlow Café at Bridgewater Monument (01442 851670); shop, Greyhound Inn (01442 851228) and Valiant Trooper (01442 851203) at Aldbury
Public transport	Train and bus services at Tring Station

This walk starts out following the Grand Union Canal northwards before climbing up past Aldbury Nowers Nature Reserve for a great view from Pitstone Hill. Then it's off through the wooded Ashridge Estate to pass the Bridgewater Monument before descending to picturesque Aldbury. From here it's a short walk back to Tring Station.

From Tring Station cross over the road, turn left, and just before the bridge turn right down to the towpath. Follow the **Grand Union Canal** (see Walk 7) northwards for 1.3km, leaving it at the bridge where you turn right along the surfaced track for 800m, crossing the railway. Cross over the road and turn right for 175m, then fork left along an enclosed bridleway. Cross the track and keep ahead (path); keep right at the split to a junction. Turn left to follow the Ridgeway up through the **Nature Reserve** and trees for 800m.

Aldbury Nowers **Nature Reserve**, originally known as Duchie's Piece, consists of two areas of chalk grassland joined by the Ridgeway. Managed by

the Hertfordshire and Middlesex Wildlife Trust, the reserve is a great place to see butterflies (the helpful information board gives pictures of many that can be seen, along with the most likely dates). The reserve is also home to glow worms – or wingless female fireflies (the males fly but do not glow) – which can be seen during summer evenings when they 'light up' a special segment in their tails to attract a mate.

Go through the gate – leaving Hertfordshire in favour of Buckinghamshire – and continue straight on, following Grim's Ditch uphill before leaving the earthwork and heading along the broad ridge of **Pitstone Hill**.

Stand on the summit of Pitstone Hill and take in the **views**: look west back along the Chiltern scarp to the Tring Reservoirs, built to supply water to the Grand Union Canal, out on the flat plain, with Aylesbury beyond; much nearer is the partly flooded chalk quarry that was once part of the Pitstone cement works between 1937 and 1991. Just to the right of the quarry is the tower of Pitstone's St Mary's Church, and further round is Pitstone windmill, with the distinctive spire of the Church of St Mary the Virgin in Ivinghoe to the north and Steps Hill and Ivinghoe Beacon (Walk 5) to the north-east.

Continue over a knoll and then down to Pitstone Hill **car park** (starting point of Walk 5). Cross the road, go through a gate and follow the right-hand fence to a cross-path junction where you turn right (Ridgeway goes straight on), still following the fence. At the next fence corner go half-right up past trees, through a gate and take the left-hand waymarked path straight on to a track. Turn right – the walk now follows the Ashridge Boundary Trail (track) for 2.6km – heading east past **Clipper Down** and then curving right (south) around Dunscombe Terrace, passing seats with distant views, and over **Moneybury Hill**.

Keep to the track, later crossing a bridge, then pass a **monument** and keep ahead across the grassy area to the visitor centre and café.

The **Bridgewater Monument** was built in 1832 to commemorate Francis Egerton, 3rd Duke of Bridgewater (1736–1803). Known as the 'father of inland navigation', he built the Bridgewater Canal in 1761 to transport coal from his mines in Lancashire. Now owned by the National Trust, on a clear day it's worth climbing the 172 steps for the extensive views.

Bear right (south-west) along the surfaced track and go straight on, keeping right at two splits, following the

The Bridgewater Monument offers a great view from the top

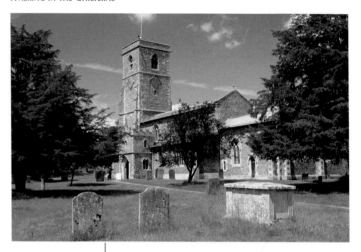

Church of St John the Baptist in Aldbury

Hertfordshire Way downhill. Ignore a crossing bridleway and continue downhill towards **Aldbury**, later passing a building to reach Toms Hill Road. Turn right to the picturesque village green and pond (just north of the pond is The Greyhound Inn, while south along Trooper Road is the Valiant Trooper). Continue straight on up Station Road, passing left of the Church of St John the Baptist.

Inside the **church**, parts of which date from the 13th century, you can see the magnificent tomb of Sir Robert Whittingham (d.1471) and his wife in the Pendley Chapel behind the stone screen.

Some 60m after the church turn right through a gate, still following the Hertfordshire Way. Continue across the field, through a gate and then alongside the buildings of **Church Farm**. Dogleg left through a gate and continue alongside the large barn, keep ahead for 400m to a cross-junction. Turn left, and at the next cross-junction go straight on, following the Ridgeway past **Westland Farm**. Bear right along the road back to **Tring Station** (ignoring a side road).

WALK 7
Grand Union Canal and Tring Park

Start/finish	Junction of Beggars Lane and Station Road at Tring Station (SP 948 120) off the A41 just east of Tring; roadside parking on Beggars Lane
Distance	12.8km (8 miles)
Ascent	230m
Time	3½hrs
Map	OS Explorer 181
Refreshments	The Greyhound (01442 824631) 600m off-route at Wigginton
Public transport	Train and bus services at Tring Station

The first part of the walk follows the peaceful Grand Union Canal southwards before crossing over at Cow Roast and following the Chiltern Way westwards, alongside Grim's Ditch, to Hastoe. The return section follows country lanes before heading along the Ridgeway through Tring Park and back to the start.

From the north end of Beggars Lane cross over Station Road, turn right across the bridge and then sharp left down to the canal. ▶ Turn sharp left, passing under the bridge, and follow the **Grand Union Canal** towards London.

To start from the railway station cross over Station Road, turn left to the bridge and fork right down to the canal.

The **Grand Union Canal**, originally known as the Grand Junction Canal, was built between 1793 and 1805 to connect England's two largest cities, London and Birmingham. It runs from Braunston to Brentford.

Follow the towpath southwards for 2.2km, passing under a bridge on the way, to reach **Cow Roast Lock**, whose name is derived from 'Cow Rest' (around here there were a number of cattle pens used by drovers to rest

The Grand Union Canal at Cow Roast Lock

animals while travelling to London from the Midlands). Leave the canal and turn right along the lane crossing the canal to reach a junction with the A4251. With care, cross over and turn right for 30m then left along take the track – signposted 'Tinker's Lodge ½' – (the walk now follows the **Chiltern Way** for 4.5km).

Keep ahead along the track to join a road beside **Tinker's Lodge**. Turn left through the A41 underpass and then right up the concrete track (signposted 'Hemp Lane ½'). This soon bears left and at the junction fork left through a gate (Chiltern Way), heading west across fields to enter Lower Wood. Continue for 50m to a junction and fork left up through the trees, pass a gate at the top and continue, soon following the left-hand hedge southwards down through the narrow field, to a minor road at **Wigginton Bottom**.

Turn left for 50m and fork right along an enclosed path – signposted 'Chesham Road ½' – as it bends right with a house on the left, later keeping ahead through trees to reach a gate and Chesham

Road (the Greyhound pub is 600m to the right from here). Turn right for 10m and then left across the road and go through a gate, continuing across the field and through another gate to a path junction. Turn right for 25m and then left, with a gorse hedge on your left. Follow the line of **Grim's Ditch** for 1.2km, later passing through a beech wood to reach a minor road. ▶

Cross over the road and enter the wood, where the path splits. Fork right, still following Grim's Ditch (right), and later leave the trees behind to continue across the field to a crossing byway (Browns Lane). Turn right for 500m to a junction in **Hastoe** and go right along Church Lane for 500m, shortly passing the village hall commissioned by Lady Emma Rothschild in 1898.

At the T-junction go left along Marlin Hill for 150m towards Tring and then fork right (Ridgeway) to enter **Tring Park**. A map shows walking routes in the park.

Grim's Ditch is the remains of a linear earthwork, thought to have originated in the Iron Age, which appears in several parts of the Chilterns hereabouts.

Tring Park, managed by the Woodland Trust, is an area of broadleaf woodland and open grassland that dates back to Norman times. To the north of the A41, which splits the park in two, is the manor house – The Mansion – designed by Sir Christopher Wren in 1682. Previous owners include Sir William Gore (Lord Mayor of London), who bought the house in 1705, and in 1872 Lionel de Rothschild bought the park as a wedding present for his son, Sir Nathaniel (later Lord) de Rothschild. The house is now home to the Tring Park School for the Performing Arts.

While walking through the park you may catch sight of the **edible dormouse** (Glis glis). These are much bigger than the native common dormouse, looking more like a small squirrel. Introduced by Lord Rothschild in 1902, the edible dormouse has been slowly spreading out across the Chilterns ever since.

The former summerhouse in Tring Park

Head northwards through Bishops Wood and then north-east, following the long straight tree-lined track – known as King Charles Ride – with Tring to the north, for 1km to a track junction (SP 931 104); along the way there are some seats on the left that give good views across Tring Park towards Tring and The Mansion. Fork left down to an obelisk known as Nell Gwynne's Monument.

From the obelisk bear half-right along the track heading north-east, going slightly uphill to reach a white-painted building (the portico and Ionic columns are all that remain of the former summerhouse). Turn sharp right, following the track uphill, and once past the gate turn sharp left along the Ridgeway and go past some houses to reach Fox Road in **Wigginton**. ▶

The route now follows the Ridgeway back to the start.

Cross over the road, go through a gate and follow the right-hand field edge past a trig point to another gate; diagonally left (north-north-east) are the Ivinghoe Hills (Walk 5). Follow the path straight on, go through a gate and turn left along the field edge before going right along the road – **The Twist** – for 20m, then turn left through a gate. Head down the enclosed path, cross the footbridge (A41) and bear right and left down an enclosed path to the **A4521** – otherwise known as Akeman Street, a former Roman Road that linked Verulamium (near St Albans) with Corinium Dobunnorum (now Cirencester).

Turn right and cross over at the traffic island before continuing alongside the road, then bear left past a gate just after Pendley Beeches Lodge. Follow the enclosed route north-eastwards for 750m – ahead you can see the Bridgewater Monument (Walk 6) on the skyline – and later turn left along Beggars Lane back to the start.

WALK 8
Great Gaddesden

Start/finish	Great Gaddesden (TL 029 112), off the A4146 north of Hemel Hempstead; roadside parking along Church Meadows
Distance	7.5km (4¾ miles)
Ascent	110m
Time	2hrs
Map	OS Explorer 182
Refreshments	Crown and Sceptre (01442 234660) off-route at Briden's Camp
Public transport	Great Gaddesden has limited bus links to Berkhamstead (excluding Sundays); Jockey End (TL 039 137 – short detour) has bus links to Hemel Hempstead

From Great Gaddesden the walk heads southwards along the valley before crossing the River Gade and climbing up past the rather grand Gaddesden Place. The route later follows an avenue of old lime trees to pass Golden Parsonage before crossing open farmland. The final section follows the Hertfordshire Way past The Hoo before descending back to Great Gaddesden.

GREAT GADDESDEN

The little village of Great Gaddesden, sitting on the banks of the River Gade whose clear waters were once used for growing watercress, was mentioned in the Domesday Book – although given that Roman bricks have been incorporated into parts of the Church of St John the Baptist, its history may go back much further. Inside the church, the early 18th-century Halsey Chapel contains an interesting collection of memorials to the Halsey family, who have lived in Great Gaddesden since the mid-15th century and who were responsible for both Gaddesden Place and the Golden Parsonage.

Leave Church Meadows heading south-east, cross Pipers Hill road diagonally rightwards and go along the track opposite, and then an enclosed path, to a field. Follow the left-hand margin to a path junction at the corner and turn left through the gate. Head south-east through the meadow, crossing the footbridge over the **River Gade**, and soon follow the fence on the left up to a gate in the corner. Pass between the buildings go right for a few metres, then go left across the road (A4146) and through the gate to pass a cottage. Continue north-east uphill, later passing through a gate and some trees before bearing slightly left. To the north-east is **Gaddesden Place**.

> The Palladian-styled **Gaddesden Place**, with its large four-columned Ionic portico with pediment, has made several TV and film appearances. Sitting on an elevated position overlooking the valley, it was originally designed by James Wyatt in 1768 for Thomas Halsey (1731–1788), with the mansion being subsequently rebuilt in 1905 following extensive fire damage.

Go through a gate and bear half-right to pass another gate. Here the path splits; keep ahead (right fork) with

Gaddesden Place

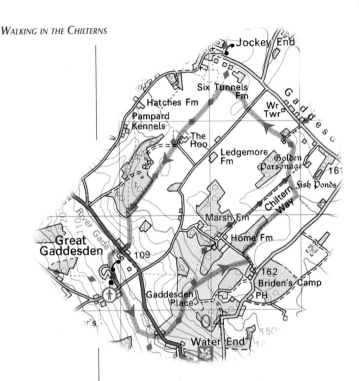

trees over to the right. Continue through three fields, passing close to Stable Wood with the Victorian-styled **Home Farm** to the left, to join a wide gravel track. (Pub visit: From here detour right, then right again, and continue along the road to reach the Crown and Sceptre pub in Briden's Camp – 450m each way.)

Turn left, and just before the trees of London Wood turn right, keeping the trees on your left. At the field corner go left and then right to continue along the avenue of lime trees to a junction (TL 049 122); turn left along the track for 175m, and at the next junction (**Chiltern Way**) turn right through a gate and bear half-left through two fields separated by a gate, passing some large trees (sweet chestnut). Over to the right is the **Golden Parsonage**.

The 18th-century red-brick **Golden Parsonage** – the name 'golden' is believed to be a corruption of 'Gaddesden' – was built for the Halsey family and is the only surviving wing of a once much larger house.

Go through a gate, follow the left-hand field edge and go through another gate. Turn left along the drive for a few metres and then turn right, with a pond on your right, to reach a gate. Bear half-left across the field and go through another gate, continuing north-westwards through two fields separated by a line of trees, later with a **water tower** to your right. Cross the lane slightly to the right and go through a gate to continue in the same direction, between fences and paddocks for 300m, to a crossing track.

Go straight on through a gate and follow the hedge and trees on the right to a crossing route. Turn left (southwest), following the Hertfordshire Way across the field. Go through a gate and keep ahead across two fields, later

Looking back along the route, which follows the Hertfordshire Way past The Hoo

The picturesque River Gade

following a track with a hedge on the left to a junction where the restricted byway goes right. Go through a gate on the left and continue straight on (south-west) past **The Hoo**, following the fence. Keep ahead through the next field and then continue down through Hoo Wood before leaving through a gate; continue southwards down across the field and follow the left-hand field edge and then a track. Cross the road (A4146), go through a gate and bear slightly right to cross footbridges over the **River Gade** before bearing slightly left. Go through a gate and keep left along the lane, with houses on the right, to get back to the start.

WALK 9

Berkhamsted, Nettleden and Little Gaddesden

Start/finish	Berkhamsted railway station (SP 993 081), or car park at north end of New Road (TL 004 092) 1.5km north-east of Berkhamsted
Distance	16.9km (10½ miles) or 12.5km (7¾ miles)
Ascent	370m or 290m
Time	5hrs or 3½hrs
Map	OS Explorer 181
Refreshments	Alford Arms (01442 864480) at Frithsden; Bridgewater Arms (01442 842408) at Little Gaddesden
Public transport	Train services to Berkhamsted

Quite a long walk, starting out from Berkhamsted and taking in parts of the Ashridge Estate as it meanders across fields and through beautiful beech woods, passing the villages of Frithsden, Nettleden and Little Gaddesden. The route, which follows parts of the Hertfordshire Way and Chiltern Way, crosses a golf course – watch out for golf balls – and offers a brief view of the Bridgewater Monument and Ashridge House (the latter can be visited by following a short detour). A shorter route, omitting Little Gaddesden, is also described.

From the railway station (northern exit) turn right, cross the road beside the bridge and follow White Hill (lane) past the entrance of **Berkhamsted Castle** to a junction.

> **Berkhamsted**, situated in the Bulbourne Valley, through which the Grand Union Canal and the mainline railway from London pass, has a place in history: it was here that the English finally surrendered to William the Conqueror in 1066. Following their success, the Normans built an important motte and bailey **castle** here to control the northern approach to London. During the Middle Ages

owners of the castle included Richard, Earl of Cornwall and the Black Prince; the castle is now a substantial ruin (open daily except Christmas Day and New Year's Day).

Go left along the pavement for 200m (roadside parking) then turn right across the road and go through a gate. Follow the line of trees uphill and turn left at the top, following the field edge through two fields. Continue along the enclosed route for 300m and turn left down through the trees (bridleway); cross the road slightly right and continue down to a cross-junction. Turn right up to a car park (TL 004 092), the alternative start.

Cross the road and pass the **war memorial**, following the way-marked bridleway across the golf course, crossing three fairways separated by trees and then continuing down through the trees. Just before the road, turn sharp left (almost doubling back) along a bridleway for 50m and then right, following an enclosed path; cross a drive and keep ahead, going down through trees to a road beside The Alford Arms in **Frithsden**.

Keep ahead and follow the lane (later unsurfaced) uphill, passing **Frithsden Vineyard**. At the brow of the hill either continue down the track or follow a parallel path in the field on the left (which offers some nice views as it descends north-eastwards to **Nettleden**).

At the T-junction, with St Lawrence's Church to the right, turn left along the road for 50m, and at the village sign fork half-right (north-west) across the field, passing a solitary tree. Continue north-westwards along the valley, ignoring a crossing track; later a path (Hertfordshire Way) joins from the right after a small copse. Go through a gate, bear half-left across the field and then go through another gate at the corner. Cross the road and go along Cromer Close. Keep ahead, following the path between houses to a path junction, and turn right between hedges to reach a play area. Bear half-left into the trees and continue downhill for 100m and then follow the track downhill to reach the valley and path junction at SP 999 122.

Picturesque cottage at Little Gaddesden

Shortcut
Head south up the grassy slope, later following a drive-way; cross the minor road, go through the trees and follow the right-hand edge of a large grassy area to rejoin the main walk at SP 990 110.

Turn right along valley (not the track) – know as Golden Valley – for 400m to reach a crossing path (yellow-topped marker post over to the left) 50m after passing a stone bridge (100m to the right). To visit **Ashridge** turn left up through the trees and follow the driveway to the house (400m each way); otherwise turn right and head up through the trees, cross a track and soon go through a gate (right) and continue along the path to the road at **Little Gaddesden**. Cross over and turn left, continuing along a surfaced path for 650m on the right-hand side of the grassy area, passing a memorial cross for Adelaide, wife of Adelbert, 3rd Earl Brownlow. Look left for a view of Ashridge House.

The history of **Ashridge** dates back to the founding of a priory by Edmund, Earl of Cornwall, in 1283 for the monastic Order of Bonhommes (or 'blue friars', due to the colour of their robes). Following Henry VIII's Dissolution of the Monasteries, Ashridge became a royal residence until it was bought in 1604 by Thomas Egerton, Lord Chancellor to Elizabeth I. Various family members became the Earls and Dukes of Bridgewater and later the Earls Brownlow. It was the 7th Earl of Bridgewater who commissioned the architect James Wyatt to design the current Neo-Gothic **Ashridge House**. Following WWI the family sold the house (now the Ashridge Business School) and the woodland estate passed to the National Trust. The gardens and parts of the house are open to the public at various times (01442 843491).

At the footpath sign ('Little Gaddesden Church ½') turn right along the track and keep ahead along the right-hand side of the playing field. Go through gates on either side of a field aiming for the church, ignore a crossing path and shortly bear left to a lane in front of the church.

Pop inside the 14th-century **Church of St Peter and St Paul** to see the lovely stained glass windows, one of which reuses 16th-century glass, and memorials to various members of the Bridgewater family from Ashridge Park.

Turn left alongside the churchyard boundary and follow an enclosed path westwards before continuing through several fields separated by gates to reach a road.

Inside the church is a monument to Elizabeth Dutton, née Egerton (d.1611), relocated from London's Church of St Martin's in the Field in 1730

Heading towards the Church of St Peter and St Paul at Little Gaddesden

Turn left, passing the village shop, and at the Bridgewater Arms turn right across the road and go through the car park. Follow the Chiltern Way, keeping ahead at a crossing driveway (footpath), then a crossing route (Ashbridge Bounday Trail) at the bottom, and head up through the trees – soon passing the golf course – and continue between houses to a drive.

Cross over and bear half-left (Chiltern Way) to a junction and follow the surfaced drive south-westwards with the golf course on your right. Near the car park bear slightly right through the trees (marker posts). Pass just right of the clubhouse, cross the fairway and head through trees, soon passing left of a large building. Follow the surfaced track past the ornate 17th-century Old Park Lodge (right). Shortly look right along the grassy ride to see the Bridgewater Monument (Walk 6), and left to Ashridge House.

Where the surfaced track curves right, continue straight on (Chiltern Way) southwards through the trees, later with an open field on your left, to reach a bridleway. Turn left, staying just inside the trees for 600m, to join a track near **Woodyard Cottages**. Turn right along the track for 450m to arrive at a junction at **Coldharbour Farm**. Go left for 150m.

Keep to the right-hand fork at the split (Hertfordshire Way); soon to your left is an open grassy area (SP 990 110 – the point at which the shortcut rejoins the main route). Keep ahead for 175m then turn right on a crossing bridleway and soon go left, following the route just inside the woodland for 1.2km, crossing a track and a waymarked route on the way. At the next crossing route (SP 998 097) go right and down through a gate, then turn left along the field edge. Keep ahead to a cross-track junction at Well Farm. Go straight through a gate, following the path alongside the right-hand hedge through three fields (not the parallel track on the other side of the hedge). Keep ahead past the cricket pitch and follow the surfaced drive to a road (Castle Hill). Bear left and continue straight on down Brownlow Road (castle on left) to the **railway station**.

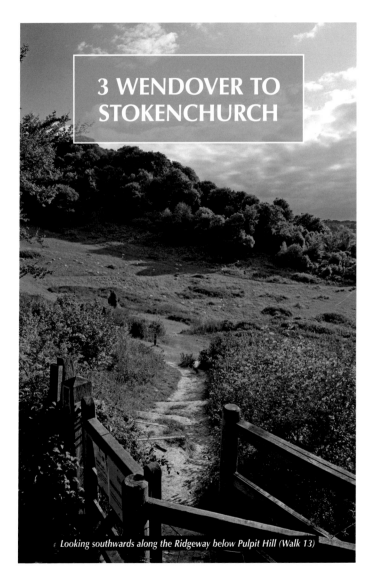

3 WENDOVER TO STOKENCHURCH

Looking southwards along the Ridgeway below Pulpit Hill (Walk 13)

WALK 10
Cholesbury and Hawridge

Start/finish	Car park at Cholesbury and Hawridge cricket ground (SP 931 071), 6km north of Chesham; signposted from A416
Distance	8.1km (5 miles)
Ascent	200m
Time	2½hrs
Maps	OS Explorer 181
Refreshments	Full Moon (01494 758959) at Cholesbury
Public transport	Limited bus services to Cholesbury and Hawridge from Chesham

An easy walk, starting out on Cholesbury Common and then, after a fleeting view of a former windmill in Hawridge, dropping down to follow a dry valley before climbing over the ridge to pass Hawridge Court. The route then heads across Hawridge Common – on the way a short detour leads to the pub at Hawridge – and then along tracks and paths through fields and woods to reach the impressive, tree-covered earthworks of Cholesbury Camp before heading back to the start.

From the car park, with the cricket ground behind you, turn left alongside the road, passing the puddingstones (left), the road to Braziers End (right) and the boundary marker (left).

The three **puddingstones** mark the spot where a beacon was lit in 2012 to celebrate Queen Elizabeth II's Diamond Jubilee, whereas the small stone obelisk on the boundary between Cholesbury and Hawridge commemorates Queen Victoria's Diamond Jubilee in 1897.

Just past The Full Moon pub, turn right alongside the hedge, cross a stile and turn left. Follow the hedge and then turn right between the fence and hedge. Cross the stile and turn left – to your right is the windmill – following the left-hand field boundary. Cross another stile and continue along two sides of the field and down to the lower left corner.

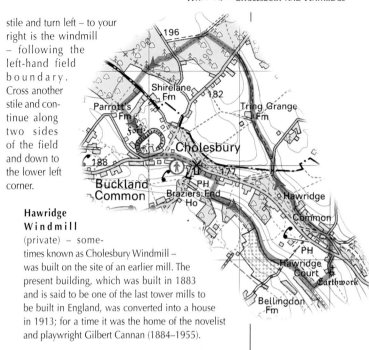

Hawridge Windmill

(private) – sometimes known as Cholesbury Windmill – was built on the site of an earlier mill. The present building, which was built in 1883 and is said to be one of the last tower mills to be built in England, was converted into a house in 1913; for a time it was the home of the novelist and playwright Gilbert Cannan (1884–1955).

The late 19th-century Hawridge Windmill

Keep ahead for a few paces to a cross junction and turn left (the walk now follows the path along the valley for 1.6km). Continue through the trees, Keeping ahead at the cross junction. Later, go through a gate (cross junction) and continue straight on through fields following the right-hand edge past another cross junction. Go straight over a track (Hawridge Lane), through a gate and keep ahead through the field. Go into the next field, following the fence and long thin wood on the right, and pass through a gate into another field.

Turn left uphill and keep ahead through two gates either side of a field, continue to the trees, and then turn left to follow the trees on your right. Just before the buildings, turn right through a gate and follow the enclosed path (with a building on the left) to join a drive at **Hawridge Court**.

The present timber-framed **Hawridge Court** stands partially on the remains of a fortified site that was probably built after the Norman Conquest (the first written evidence of it dates from the 13th century). The adjacent St Mary's Church was extensively rebuilt in the 19th century.

Turn left along the drive past the church and soon head down to a T-junction. Cross the road and head half-left down through the trees before bearing left along the lane. Keep left at the junction and just after the houses on the left, where the lane starts to rise, fork right along a track signposted 'Hawridge Vale'.

Follow the track for 400m, and where this turns right (last house) go straight on through the trees for 450m, keeping close to the lower edge of **Hawridge Common**. Bear right along the road for 125m and then fork left along the surfaced driveway towards **Tring Grange Farm**. Keep right (straight on) at the farm, following the track; later cross the road to enter a wood where the path splits. Take the left fork (signposted 'Shire Lane ¾') and soon bear half-right, following an old boundary bank and line of trees heading north-west, to the far side of the wood.

Do not go through the gate – instead stay in the wood and turn left (south-west) for 350m.

Cross a minor road and continue through the trees opposite. Keep ahead at a crossing byway, go through a gate and continue alongside the left-hand field hedge. Exit through a gate, go left along the lane for 20m and then right on a path between a track (left) and a house and garden (right). Keep to the path with a wood on your right for 350m to a cross-path junction and turn left through a gate. Follow the right-hand field edge, go through a gate and keep ahead close to the right-hand edge of the wood. Keep to the right-hand path at the split (straight on), later go through a gate and continue to reach the earthworks of a **fort**.

> The impressive earthworks of **Cholesbury Camp** date from the Iron Age; excavations in the 1930s uncovered fragments of handmade pottery. Located within the earthworks is St Lawrence's Church, which was extensively restored in the 1870s.

Turn right and follow the earthworks anti-clockwise to a gravel drive (to the left is St Lawrence's Church). Turn right onto the lane, then left and left again, and follow the road back to the start.

The walk passes the tree-shaded earthworks of Cholesbury Camp – a former Iron Age fort

WALK 11

Wendover and The Lee

Start/finish	Clock tower in Wendover at the junction of High Street and the B4009 (SP 869 078 – parking nearby), or Wendover railway station (SP 865 077)
Distance	14.1km (8¾ miles)
Ascent	340m
Time	4¼hrs
Maps	OS Explorer 181
Refreshments	Pubs, shops and cafés in Wendover; The Old Swan (01494 837239) at Swan Bottom; Cock and Rabbit Inn (01494 837540) at The Lee
Public transport	Wendover has good bus and train links

A fairly long, hilly walk from Wendover, climbing the Chiltern escarpment to pass through Wendover Woods and visit the picturesque countryside around The Lee – home to a rather unusual sight. The return route follows the Chiltern Link back to Wendover. This walk can be easily split into two shorter walks by following the well-signposted Ridgeway National Trail between SP 895 070 and SP 881 063.

Anyone starting from the railway station should turn right along Station Approach, then left down Pound Street and High Street to the clock tower.

◀ From the 19th-century clock tower (originally built as a market hall and lock-up) head north-east along the road for Tring and Halton (B4009) for 250m, passing the thatched Coldharbour Cottages and The Packhorse pub, using the right-hand pavement. Fork right at the junction, keep ahead parallel to the main road and shortly turn right up Colet Road then left along Barlow Road. At the corner, go straight on along Beechwood Lane to its end. Bear right up a path, go over a crossing route and then steeply up **Boddington Hill**, part of Wendover Woods.

This large open access **wood**, managed by the Forestry Commission, has waymarked trails and a

WENDOVER

Coldharbour ('Anne Boleyn') Cottages in Wendover

The historic market town of Wendover sits in a gap in the Chiltern Hills that gave an easier route for stagecoaches travelling between London and the Midlands; a number of old coaching inns remain, including the Red Lion on High Street. In 1796 the Wendover Arm of the Grand Union Canal was built, connecting Wendover to the main canal at Bulbourne. Unfortunately, due to water leakage the canal closed in 1901. The railway arrived in 1892, making use of the easy route through the chalk escarpment and offering services to London. But much earlier than all of these were the Icknield Way and Ridgeway, which travelled along the higher ground.

The picturesque Coldharbour Cottages (also known as Anne Boleyn's Cottages) on Tring Road – or more likely the land on which they stand – are reputed to have been a wedding present given to Anne Boleyn by Henry VIII.

café; hidden amongst the trees on Boddington Hill are the remains of an Iron Age hill fort.

At the top bear left along the track for 100m, then right following a track (footpath) downhill, keeping left at the split; soon (50m) on the left is a wildlife hide and to

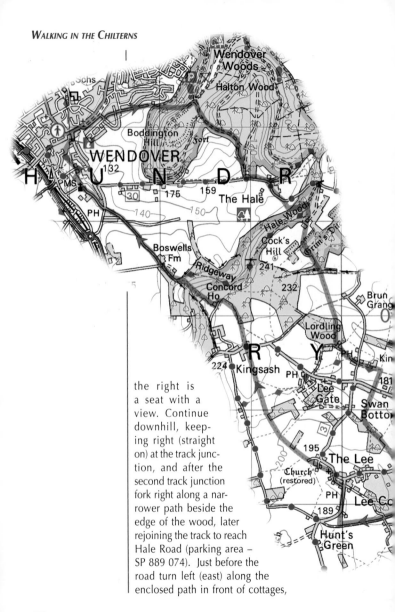

the right is a seat with a view. Continue downhill, keeping right (straight on) at the track junction, and after the second track junction fork right along a narrower path beside the edge of the wood, later rejoining the track to reach Hale Road (parking area – SP 889 074). Just before the road turn left (east) along the enclosed path in front of cottages, keeping parallel with the lane, heading through trees and a field to rejoin the lane beside Hale Farm Cottage.

Follow the lane south for 200m passing Hale Farmhouse and **The Hale** and then turn half-right through a gate and keep ahead, up across the field to enter **Hale Wood**. Here the path splits; fork left uphill and keep ahead across the Ridgeway (SP 895 070), soon leaving the trees and passing a house.

Continue along the left-hand field margin and then straight on across the field to enter the wood, crossing **Grim's Ditch** (visible on both sides). Keep ahead at the junction and follow the left-hand field edge. Go through the trees and continue across the next field. Keep ahead through more trees and head south-south-east across the large field. Pass through the hedge (crossing bridleway) and continue across the next field. Follow the path southwards through **Lordling Wood** to a five-way junction. Bear left (almost straight on) along the track (byway), passing a house and keep to the track for 300m to a road beside The Old Swan pub.

Turn right for a few metres, then left through a gate (Chiltern Way) between fences to another gate. Turn right down the bridleway, cross the road at **Swan Bottom** and follow the driveway opposite (Kingsvale Farm), keeping left. Go through a gate and continue along the left side of the fields to a path junction in the trees. Turn left for 400m, later ignoring a path to the right and one to the left, and enter a field. Take the right-hand fork across the field and continue alongside the fence to a road junction in **Lee Clump** (to the right is the village shop).

Keep ahead (Oxford Street) and immediately after the school turn right along the track and go through a gate. Keep slightly left and downhill, passing just to the right of some trees, and go through another gate (to your right is an attractive cottage surrounded by a hedge). Follow the path as it curves right to a crossing surfaced track and keep ahead for 500m.

Picturesque cottage at Lee Common

Turn right over a stile beside a stable, follow the enclosed track to a minor road and turn right towards The Lee, passing the entrance to Pipers (private house) and a statue.

An unexpected sight: the bow figurehead at Pipers

The statue, a **bow figurehead** from HMS Howe (later renamed HMS Impregnable) representing Admiral Earl Howe, the leader of the Channel Fleet during the French Revolutionary Wars, must be one of the strangest sights in the Chilterns. As for how it came to be land-locked here is down to London's famous Liberty department store, founded by Sir Arthur Lasenby Liberty from nearby Chesham – who also built Pipers. The oak timbers from the ship were used in the 1920s to build the Tudor-style frontage of the store on Great Marlborough Street (London), while the figurehead was placed here at Pipers.

At the junction, beside the Cock and Rabbit Inn, turn left (keeping left of the green) to reach another junction. Go left along the road for 50m and then left through a gate into the churchyard.

Attractive cottages surround the village green at **The Lee**, which has starred in several episodes of ITV's *Midsomer Murders*. As well as the pub, there are a couple of churches dedicated to St John the Baptist; the first is a red-brick Victorian structure, while behind this is the original 13th-century church.

Follow the path past both churches and bear right to cross a stile. Turn left alongside the wall and cross stiles either side of a driveway to enter a field where the path splits. (The walk now follows the Chiltern Link for 4.9km back to Wendover.) Fork right across the field and cross a stile. The path splits again, take the right-hand fork (Chiltern Link) into the right-hand fieldand continue alongside the hedge on the left. Pass the end of a belt of trees and keep ahead, now with the hedge on the right, through a couple of fields. At the field corner on the far side of the second field go left for 40m, then go right through a hedge-gap to continue alongside the right-hand hedge, ignoring the crossing Chiltern Way. Cross a stile at the corner and head slightly left through the field to cross another stile. Cross the track, go through a gate and turn left along the drive to reach a road in **Kingsash**.

Cross over, keep ahead through two gates (house on left) and continue alongside the left-hand field margin. Cross the stile at the field corner and follow the the right-hand boundary along two sides of the field. Turn right over a stile and head north-west past **Concord House** (house on left). Pass a gate and head down through the trees, later with a sunken bridleway on the left, to a junction (SP 881 063) with the Ridgeway, which is also now followed back to Wendover.

Follow the track – Hogtrough Lane – ahead for 1.1km passing passing **Boswells Farm** and Wellhead Farm. Keep ahead at the junction beside Wellhead Cottage, following the lane to the Church of St Mary the Virgin (left).

Although established in the 12th century, the present building of the **Church of St Mary the Virgin** is mostly 14th century with Victorian restorations.

The final stage of the route meanders alongside a stream back to the centre of Wendover

Inside is an interesting array of carvings, including human heads along with fruit, flowers and animals on the capitals of the pillars.

Turn right along the Heron Path, with Hampden Pond on the left, and bear right to follow the surfaced path (Ridgeway) past a cottage and then alongside a stream on the right, passing Rope Walk flower meadow and Memorial Community Orchard. Keep ahead and continue back to the clock tower.

WALK 12

Wendover, Ellesborough, Chequers
and Coombe Hill

Start/finish	Clock tower in Wendover at the junction of the High Street and B4009 (SP 869 078 – parking nearby), or Wendover railway station (SP 865 077)
Distance	12km (7½ miles)
Ascent	295m
Time	3½hrs
Maps	OS Explorer 181
Refreshments	Pubs, cafés and shops in Wendover; Russell Arms (01296 624411) off-route at Butlers Cross
Public transport	Wendover has good bus and train links

This walk heads south-west, below the chalk scarp, from Wendover to the little village of Ellesborough before climbing up the side of Beacon Hill. After skirting around Chequers – the Prime Minister's country residence – the route follows the Ridgeway up over Coombe Hill and back to Wendover.

Walk up the High Street and Pound Street, passing Station Approach on the right. ▶ After crossing the bridge, but before the houses, turn right on a track signposted 'Aylesbury Ring'. Keep right at the split, continue alongside the boundary and then head half-left (north-west) across the field and through a gate (this path arrangement may change due to the HS2 rail link). Continue southwest through paddocks separated by gates before bearing right along an old field boundary towards **Wellwick Farm**. Just before the cottages turn left and then right, continue north-westwards between the large barn (left) and cottages (right). Go through the gate and bear half-left across two fields, passing just right of Wellwick House and later following the left-hand fence. Cross the stile and keep ahead over another stile, then continue through the middle of two fields to a cross-path junction.

Anyone starting from the railway station joins here.

85

Heading south-west from Wellwick Farm towards Butler's Cross below the Chiltern escarpment

In the next field follow the left-hand margin, then continue along the enclosed track and go through the next field to a gate. Cross the road, turn left towards **Butlers Cross** and continue for 50m with cottages on your left, then turn right through a gate. (To visit the Russell Arms pub continue along the road for 250m; return by retracing your steps and turning left.) Follow the narrow path and later go straight on to a lane at Springs Farm. Keep ahead to the thatched Springs Cottage at the end and go through the gate. Keep ahead alongside the fence (left) for 40m to a junction and turn left up through the field towards the church in **Ellesborough** (the attractive Church of St Peter and St Paul, with its tall crenellated tower,

dates mainly from the 15th century). Continue up through the churchyard, past the church, and leave via the gate.

Cross the road and turn right along the raised path, then go left through a gate. Head south-south-west up across the field, through a gate, and continue skirting up the right-hand slope of **Beacon Hill** (open access land) to reach a gate. To your right are the earthworks of a former motte and bailey castle known as **Cymbeline's Castle**.

Follow the path and steps through wooded Ellesborough Warren. ▶ Continue across the field to a gate and keep ahead through the trees, ignoring a crossing track, to go through a gate into a field. Follow the fence with Whorley Wood on the left and go through a gate at the corner. (The walk now follows the Ridgeway

This deep coombe, along with those at Great Kimble and Little Kimble, is one of a handful of sites in Britain where box (*Buxus sempervirens*) grows naturally.

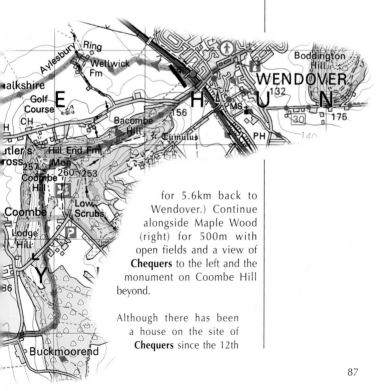

for 5.6km back to Wendover.) Continue alongside Maple Wood (right) for 500m with open fields and a view of **Chequers** to the left and the monument on Coombe Hill beyond.

Although there has been a house on the site of **Chequers** since the 12th century, little is known about it. The present, imposing mansion was restored and enlarged in the 16th century by Sir William Hawtrey, who guarded a royal prisoner – Lady Jane Grey – at the house for two years. Jump forward to the 19th century and the house was remodelled in a Gothic Revival style (or Victorian Gothic) for the Russell family. It was later bought by Lord Lee of Fareham and his wife Ruth, who immediately set about removing the earlier changes to give the house its present appearance. Lord Lee later gave the house to the nation for use as the official country residence of the Prime Minister.

At the corner of the wood turn left through a gate, following the posts downhill, and go through gates either side of the tree-lined driveway that leads to Chequers (to the right are the twin gatehouses). Keep ahead, passing a stand of trees to reach a gate and road. Cross over and take the track opposite, staying left of the houses.

Chequers – the Prime Minister's country residence

Keep straight on at the crossing bridleway, following the Ridgeway up through Goodmerhill Wood. Once the path has levelled out, go left at the signpost and head in a northerly direction (the path can be indistinct at times but there are several Ridgeway marker posts). When a field becomes visible to the right, dogleg right through a fence-gap and continue northwards, close to the edge of the wood on the right, to a road.

Turn right up the road for 100m to a house on the right. Go left through the trees to a gate and National Trust sign for Coombe Hill; turn down to the left for 25m and once past the trees go right, keeping the slope down to your left and the trees and scrub to your right, to reach the monument on **Coombe Hill**.

> At 260m, **Coombe Hill** is one of the highest points in the Chilterns (with Haddington Hill, in Wendover Woods, taking the title at 267m). Its monument, built in 1904, is a memorial to the Buckinghamshire soldiers who died during the Boer War (1899–1902). On a clear day the view includes, from left to right: nearby Chequers (SSW) and Beacon Hill (SW) with the Chiltern scarp beyond; distant Wittenham Clumps (31km WSW); Ellesborough Church (W); Brill Hill (20km WNW); Waddesdon Manor (15km NW); Aylesbury (N); and the wooded slopes at Bow Brickhill near Milton Keynes (28km NNE). Coombe Hill was donated to the National Trust by Lord Lee of Fareham in 1918.

Turn right (east-north-east) along a broad grassy path between two lines of scrub (**not** the gravel path). Go through gates either side of a sunken bridleway and keep ahead over **Bacombe Hill** – a local nature reserve noted for its orchids and butterflies. Later, fork slightly left to keep to the main path (Ridgeway), descending beside a ditch on the right. ▶ Continue downhill, leave through a gate and pass a small parking area, cross the road and turn right back to **Wendover**.

Ahead are views of Wendover and Halton House – a late 19th-century mansion that was built for Alfred de Rothschild and has featured in TV and film productions.

WALK 13
Whiteleaf Hill and Great Kimble

Start/finish	Whiteleaf Hill car park (SP 822 036) 1.2km south-west of A4010 at Monks Risborough, or Monks Risborough railway station (SP 809 048), 400m off the route
Distance	8km (5 miles)
Ascent	250m
Time	2½hrs
Maps	OS Explorer 181
Refreshments	Red Lion (01844 344476) off-route at Whiteleaf; Three Crowns (01844 347166) at Askett
Public transport	Bus and train links to Monks Risborough (short detour)

Having admired the views from Whiteleaf Hill, the walk drops down to Monks Risborough and passes the picture-postcard thatched cottages of Askett before reaching Great Kimble. Here a short detour leads to the church in Little Kimble, famed for its wall paintings. The return route heads up towards Pulpit Hill and then through wooded countryside back to Whiteleaf Hill. The walk may be started at nearby Monks Risborough railway station, adding 1km to the total distance.

From the railway station, turn right along Crowbrook Road then left along Mill Lane for 400m. Just after Courtmoor Close turn left on a signed path to join the main route at SP 812 045.

◄ Follow the path from the far end of the car park (passing the information boards) and then bear right (northwards) along the Ridgeway, shortly passing a gate and Neolithic burial mound, to reach a signpost on Whiteleaf Hill. To the left is a great view out over the **Whiteleaf Cross**.

> This unusual chalk hill **carving** – a triangle topped with a cross – above Princes Risborough was first mentioned in the 18th century. As for its purpose, no-one is really sure.

Continue northwards, following the Icknield Way (bridleway); go through a gate and head downhill to a fenced water reservoir. Bear right (lane on right) and then immediately go left, following a bridleway alongside the fence on the left. Continue downhill, and follow the driveway between houses to reach a road in **Whiteleaf**. Turn left and then right down The Holloway (to visit The Red Lion pub keep straight on for 75m; return by retracing your steps and turning left). After the driveway on the left, fork left through a gate an follow the enclosed path, go through

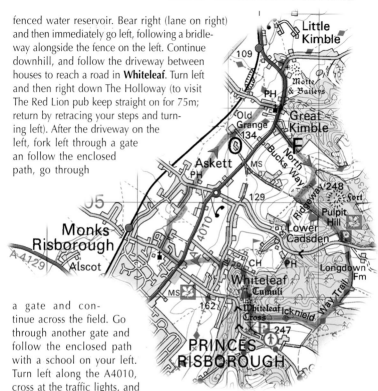

a gate and continue across the field. Go through another gate and follow the enclosed path with a school on your left. Turn left along the A4010, cross at the traffic lights, and shortly go right along Mill Lane in **Monks Risborough** for 200m to reach a footpath sign on the right (SP 812 045). ▶ A short detour left across the road leads to St Dunstan's Church.

If starting from the station, join the walk here.

Inside the church is a **sculpture** of St Dunstan, based on the legend of his encounter with Satan, by local sculptor Maureen Coatman. Just to the southwest of the church, in the adjacent park, is a 16th-century dovecote.

The painted screen inside St Dunstan's Church at Monks Risborough

The Three Crowns pub at Askett

To continue on the main route, turn right along the enclosed path, soon bearing left around a building. Cross a footbridge, go through a gate and head diagonally across the field to a plank bridge in the far corner. Go through the gate, continue through two narrow fields (crossing a stile) and then go through another gate. Follow the tree-shaded path to a junction and turn left alongside the brick wall, then turn right along the lane through **Askett**, passing its delightful thatched cottages to reach a T-junction.

Go right, cross over to the Three Crowns pub and take the signed path through the gate just right of the buildings. The path splits, follow the right-hand enclosed path and go through a gate; keep straight on through three fields separated by gates, and at the corner of the third field go right over the stile. Here the path splits: take the left fork (north-east) across the field to a further stile, then cross the garden and driveway to a gate.

Continue through the field, cross the stile and take the left fork (straight on), heading north-east, staying near the left-hand fence. Soon join a track and pass a stile and pond (left). Continue through the field, crossing another stile, and then pass a gate, and down some steps. Turn right up Church Lane in **Great Kimble** to reach a T-junction with the A4010 and turn right; on your right is St Nicholas Church.

It was at a meeting in 1635 at St Nicholas Church in Great Kimble that **John Hampden** (see Walk 16), known as 'The Patriot', refused to pay Ship Money – a tax imposed by Charles I – starting a chain of events that ultimately led to the Civil War.

Detour to Little Kimble and All Saints Church

Turn left alongside the A4010 for 400m, cross over just before the junction and go a short way along Ellesborough Road (signposted for Wendover and Butlers Cross) to reach the church on the right. Retrace your steps.

The church where John Hampden refused to pay Ship Money, leading to the Civil War

Take a short detour to see the 14th-century wall painting of St George in Little Kimble's church

All Saints Church features some remarkable religious wall paintings, including St George and St Francis preaching to the birds. It also contains a Norman font, some 13th-century floor tiles and fragments of medieval glass.

Cross the road at the bus stop and continue southwards for a few metres before forking left up the track (signposted for the Ridgeway, North Bucks Way and Pulpit Hill). After 700m, at a Ridgeway sign (the North Bucks Way starts here – it's 35 miles to Wolverton), turn right down some steps, go through a gate and follow the Ridgeway south-south-west for 300m through BBOWTs Grangelands Nature Reserve.

Go through a gate and turn left, heading south-east along the bridleway for 700m with **Pulpit Hill** up to the left. Pass behind a small car park and soon turn right across the road, following the Icknield Way (bridleway). Keep ahead at a crossing path in a dip, and at the next junction turn right for a few metres and then left (bridleway), going gently uphill for 200m to reach a cross-junction. Turn right (Icknield Way), keeping near the edge of the wood on the left for 700m, to reach a gravel path (Ridgeway). Turn left for 175m and fork left back to the **car park**.

WALK 14
Bledlow and Radnage

Start/finish	Chinnor Hill nature reserve car park, south-east of Chinnor (SP 766 002)
Distance	12.8km (8 miles)
Ascent	420m
Time	4hrs
Maps	OS Explorer 171 and 181 (just)
Refreshments	Lions of Bledlow (01844 343345) at Bledlow; The Boot (01494 481499) at Bledlow Ridge
Public transport	Bus links to Chinnor Hill and Bledlow Ridge from Oxford and High Wycombe

From Chinnor Hill Nature Reserve the route heads down to the attractive village of Bledlow – used as the setting for several TV programmes, including *Midsomer Murders* and *Miss Marple*, and home to a pub, historic church and a tranquil waterside garden. From here it continues to Lodge Hill (with some great views) before returning via Bledlow Ridge and visiting the church at Radnage.

From the back of the car park follow the level bridleway signposted 'Chinnor Barrows 400m' (not the surfaced track heading downhill), going north-eastwards through the trees and passing a map of the Chinnor Hill Nature Reserve, to reach a gate on the left after 350m. ▶ Here, either keep ahead and follow the fence or go through the gate and follow the permitted path as it meanders northwards, passing a couple of seats offering great views, before passing another gate to rejoin the main path.

The reserve contains a mix of chalk grassland and scrub, with plants such as juniper, rock rose, pyramidal and twayblade orchid. The adjacent Chinnor Hill Barrows date from the Bronze Age.

Continue downhill, following the fence on the left and later using the footpath above and left of the sunken bridleway. Turn right along the Ridgeway to a junction beside a house (right) at **Hempton Wainhill** and go straight on down the track (Midshires Way and Swan's

Way). Where the track curves right and starts to rise, go straight on, following a grassy strip across the field towards **Bledlow**. (Just to the north of here is the Chinnor and Princes Risborough Railway. Part of the line, which opened in 1872, now operates as a heritage railway using both steam and diesel hauled trains. (Talking timetable: 01844 353535; general information: www.chinnorrailway.co.uk)

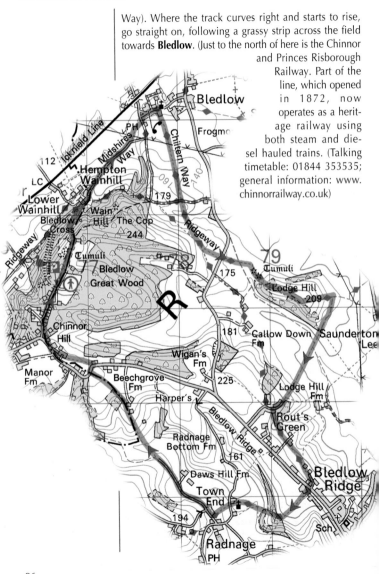

The Early English-styled Holy Trinity Church in **Bledlow** dates from the 12th and 13th centuries; inside is a Norman font and the remains of some medieval wall paintings. Just to the east are the tranquil Lyde Gardens (open daily), based around the springs that form the River Lyde, and across the road is the 17th- and 18th-century Manor House, the estate has been in the Carrington family since the 1790s.

Pass in front of The Lions of Bledlow pub, heading along the road (Church End) for 150m before turning right at the Chiltern Way sign and following the enclosed path between houses to a gate. (To visit the church and water gardens continue along the road; both are on the left, with the gardens slightly further on.)

Follow the left-hand margin through two fields and then go through gates either side of a track. Continue down across the next field, passing through a belt of trees before heading uphill. Go through gates either side of a

Following the Midshires Way and Swan's Way down to Bledlow

line of trees and turn left along the **Ridgeway**, following the fence and trees on the left. Go through a gate close to the field corner and turn right along the right-hand field edge (shortly the Chiltern Way forks right). Cross the road diagonally left, go through a gate and follow the Ridgeway through two fields, keeping ahead at a crossing track, to reach a gate in the far hedge. Turn right along enclosed path and then continue up through the trees of **Lodge Hill**, later following a fence on the left with some lovely views.

Keep ahead through a gate and continue through trees and scrub for 300m to pass a seat with more views. At the fence turn left, steeply downhill – the views from here ahead include the Lacey Green windmill (Walk 15). Go through a gate and leave the Ridgeway by turning right through a hedge-gap and follow the level bridleway south-westwards for 400m to a field.

Go straight on, following the right-hand field edge, and in the next field keep ahead to a gate and follow the fenced bridleway up towards **Rout's Green**. Keep ahead

The view to the east towards Lacey Green windmill from Lodge Hill

St Mary's Church – at Radnage

through a gate and follow the lane for 150m, then turn left beside a telegraph pole and follow the narrow path (the route now follows the Chiltern Way to Radnage). Go through a gate and follow the left-hand field margin down to a dip, then go up through a gate. Continue along the enclosed path, then cross the track and follow the enclosed path – later with views to the left. Cross a stile and soon continue along the track as it bears right to a road in **Bledlow Ridge** (to the right is The Boot pub).

Cross over and follow the enclosed path down to a wood. Turn right through the trees to reach a gate, follow the meandering path past areas of scrub and start heading down towards **Radnage**, eventually following trees on the left at the bottom to reach a gate. ▶ Head half-right through three fields, aiming for the church in the trees, and follow the path through the churchyard, passing left of the church.

This area forms part of BBOWTs Yoesden Bank nature reserve offering a mix of chalk grassland and beach woodland with a range of butterflies and plants.

The beautiful early 13th-century **St Mary's Church** in Radnage (which may have been built by the Knights Templar, who were granted the manor by King John) displays late Norman and early English architecture, including three original lancet windows. Inside there are fragments of medieval wall paintings and post-Reformation religious texts. The church doubled as 'Cranford Church' in the BBC TV series *Cranford*, and was one of the main settings in the 1987 film *A Month in the Country*.

Head down the drive, cross the lane and go through a gate (Chiltern Way). Keep ahead through the field to another gate, go straight on across the driveway and shortly turn right along the lane. As the lane bends left (Sprigs Holly Lane) and climbs, fork right (straight on) along the surfaced track for 450m, and where this bends right towards Daws Hill Farm fork left along the hedge-lined bridleway for 350m to a path junction. Cross a stile on the right, head diagonally over the field and cross another stile. Follow the right-hand boundary up through the next field, cross a stile and continue through the trees. Keep ahead, following the right-hand field edge to the top right corner. Turn right along the road (verge on right) and at the right-hand bend turn left across the road and follow the track towards Badgers View Farm.

Keep to the enclosed path past the farm buildings and continue through a small field. Leave through a gate in the corner; bear right along the road (Red Lane), passing a bus stop, and turn right along Hill Top Lane for 550m back to the **car park**.

WALK 15
Lacey Green, Speen and Bryant's Bottom

Start/finish	The Whip Inn, Lacey Green (SP 818 006); roadside parking along Pink Road
Distance	12.1km (7½ miles)
Ascent	295m
Time	3½hrs
Maps	OS Explorer 181 and 172
Refreshments	The Whip Inn (01844 344060) at Lacey Green; shop at Speen; The Gate (01494 488632) at Bryant's Bottom; Hampden Arms (01494 488255) off-route at Great Hampden
Public transport	Regular bus links from High Wycombe and Aylesbury to Lacey Green

This walk starts out high up in the Chiltern Hills at Lacey Green – home to an impressive windmill – and heads across open countryside to Speen. From here it's off past Upper North Dean and Bryant's Bottom before heading through the wooded landscapes of Hampden Common and Monkton Wood. The final section follows the Chiltern Way back to Lacey Green.

The **windmill** at Lacey Green, parts of which date back to the 1650s, has been lovingly restored from a near-derelict state by volunteers from The Chiltern Society, and is believed to be the oldest smock mill in the country. A smock mill has a top section that rotates so that the sails can be aligned with the wind direction. (For opening times and further information go to www.laceygreenwindmill.org.uk)

At the crossroads, with the windmill and The Whip Inn behind you, turn left and follow the road (Main Road) south-east through **Lacey Green** for 300m. Turn left along Goodacres Lane and keep ahead along the track, then

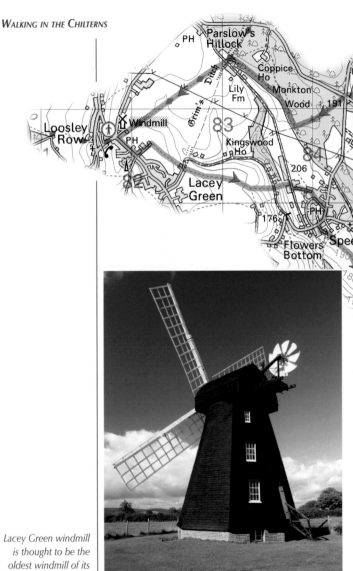

Lacey Green windmill is thought to be the oldest windmill of its kind in the country

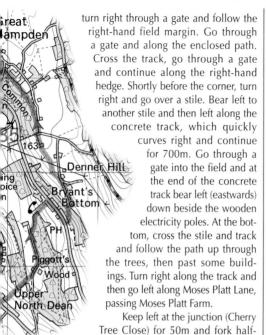

turn right through a gate and follow the right-hand field margin. Go through a gate and along the enclosed path. Cross the track, go through a gate and continue along the right-hand hedge. Shortly before the corner, turn right and go over a stile. Bear left to another stile and then left along the concrete track, which quickly curves right and continue for 700m. Go through a gate into the field and at the end of the concrete track bear left (eastwards) down beside the wooden electricity poles. At the bottom, cross the stile and track and follow the path up through the trees, then past some buildings. Turn right along the track and then go left along Moses Platt Lane, passing Moses Platt Farm.

Keep left at the junction (Cherry Tree Close) for 50m and fork half-right along a narrow path between houses at **Speen**. Turn left along Studridge Lane and then right at the T-junction along Hampden Road, to reach a junction beside the village sign opposite the village store.

Turn right along Chapel Hill for 100m, then left along Water Lane, later passing a house (Two Stiles). Once in the field (four-way junction) keep ahead alongside the fence, go through a gate at the corner and continue straight on towards the trees. Bear right down the left-hand field margin, passing through two more fields, and continue alongside the barn to a road in **Upper North Dean**.

Bear right for 150m, then go left between houses and up the left-hand field margin to the top left corner. Turn left over the stile and then right to continue up through the trees for 190m to a surfaced drive. Bear left for 450m,

The Speen village sign

passing Pigotts, and at the end (private house ahead) turn right into the trees and immediately fork left, soon heading downhill.

> **Pigotts** was once the home of sculptor, printer, writer and designer Eric Gill (1882–1940), who made a number of Art Deco sculptures including some for the BBC's Broadcasting House (London) and the Midland Hotel (Morecambe). He also designed several typefaces including Gill Sans and Perpetua. Gill is buried at the early 19th-century brick and flint church just off Chapel Hill in Speen.

Leave the trees behind and continue down towards **Bryant's Bottom**, keeping close to the right-hand hedge. Go through the gate, turn right along the road for 300m and just before The Gate pub turn left. Follow the path as it bears left above gardens and then right up to a track (bridleway).

Turn left past a house and continue past buildings at **Denner Hill**, and on joining a lane beside a cottage turn left through a gate. Head half-right over the field, go through a gate and then turn right, following the top of the field and passing power lines. Pass through a gate and continue towards the buildings. Cross the stile near the left-hand field corner and continue past Denner Farm, following the track as it bends right. At the next right bend go left through a gate and follow a path northwards through the trees of **Hampden Common**, keeping close to the right-hand edge of the wood for 200m. After passing a house visible through the trees on the right, fork left (north-north-west) to a junction and fork left again (almost straight on), later passing a line of wooden electricity poles. Keep straight on through the trees, cross a stile and continue along the track to a road.

Go left down the road for 75m, then right and up through a gate to continue through the trees of Hampden Coppice. Keep ahead at a cross-junction and head gently downhill to a path junction and gate. (To visit the Hampden Arms, turn right uphill and continue alongside

*The route through
Hampden Coppice*

the cricket pitch to a crossroads and the pub. Retrace
route – 800m return.)

Turn right along the road to a crossroads and turn
half-left between Hampden Road and Bryant's Bottom
Road, heading south-westwards up through **Monkton
Wood** for 300m. Go straight over a track and continue
for 375m to reach a crossing path at the far side of the
wood. Turn right, staying just inside the wood for 1km
and later passing close to **Lily Farm**. At the path junction,
bear left past Iron Beech Cottage and go left along the
lane for 20m (some 500m to the right along the lane is
the Pink & Lily pub at Parslow's Hillock, frequented by
the World War 1 poet Robert Brooke while walking in
the Chilterns).

Turn right up beside the house (the walk now follows
the Chiltern Way back to Lacey Green) and after 100m
fork right into a field and continue diagonally across the
corner to a gate in the hedge. Keep ahead across the
next field, passing just right of the pylon; cross the stile
and follow the fenced track between paddocks, keeping
straight on at two cross-junctions. Turn right over the stile
and head half-left (west) across the small field to a gate.
Continue through the next field, later following a hedge
on the right, and then continue through two more fields
to the road. Turn right to go back to the start.

WALK 16

Great Hampden

Start/finish	Small layby opposite a house (The Old Post Office), 300m south-east of Hampden Arms pub along Memorial Road in Great Hampden (SP 847 013)
Distance	8.7km (5½ miles)
Ascent	185m
Time	2½hrs
Map	OS Explorer 181
Refreshments	Hampden Arms (01494 488255) at Great Hampden
Public transport	Very limited bus service from High Wycombe

This short walk meanders through the lovely wooded countryside around Great Hampden, passing Hampden Bottom and Little Hampden. On the way, stop off to see a memorial to John Hampden as well as taking in a view of Hampden House and calling in at the adjacent church.

Facing the house, turn right (south-east) and go alongside the road down to a junction (more roadside parking to the right – SP 849 011). Fork left (straight on) along School Lane. Follow the road as it bends left and right to a junction and keep right for 200m. Turn left along a track towards the Old Rectory, and just before the gate go left along the enclosed path (not the bridleway). Cross a stile and keep ahead past a tree to a path junction just past bushes on the right. Turn right, following the hedge on the right, and continue down through the trees.

Cross the road and go up through the trees, soon going left into the field and then right to follow the trees (right) uphill. Keep ahead into the next field, following the right-hand fence towards **Honor End Farm**. At the far side of the field turn right along the bridleway, leave the field and turn left along Honor End Lane for 300m, passing Honor Lodge.

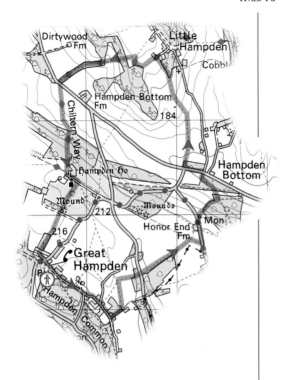

Just past the **monument** go right through a gate and follow a path down across the field towards the trees.

The stone **cross**, or 'Ship Money Memorial', commemorates John Hampden (1594–1643), one-time MP for Wendover, who refused to pay Charles I's unpopular ship money tax on some of his land – one of the events that led to the Civil War. Statues of this great 17th-century Parliamentarian can be seen at Aylesbury's Market Square and in the House of Commons, London.

Follow the path down through Pepperboxes Wood (cared for by the Woodland Trust), keeping close to the left-hand edge to reach a cross-path junction where you turn left. Cross stiles either side of the long grassy strip known as The Glade, with distant views of Hampden House (left) and two lodge houses (right), known as the Pepper Pots. Follow the path down through the trees, keeping left at the marker post, to join a road at the lower left corner of the wood. ◄

Just to the right is a small thatched cottage and the Little Hampden Forge with some interesting ironwork on display.

Turn left along the road for 200m (verge on left), and after the junction with Glade Road turn right across the road and follow the path along a line of wooden pylons, with trees on the right for a while. Keep alongside the left-hand field edge for 250m and then dogleg left through the hedge to continue uphill with the open field now on your left, heading towards **Little Hampden**, later continue just inside the wood. Go straight on along the track and just before Warren Cottage go left, following the **Chiltern Way**. At the T-junction turn right into the field and follow the left edge to the corner, then go right to a marker post.

Distinctive Hampden House

Turn left down through the trees and gate to an open field with a handily placed seat – a great place for a rest.

Continue west and down across the fields, aiming for the trees, and turn left down through them to reach a gate. Cross the road and follow the path (Chiltern Way) opposite, heading diagonally left up across the field. Continue up through the trees to a gate and then head south across the field, with a great view of **Hampden House** to the left.

> Although parts of **Hampden House** date from the 14th century, the core of the present building is Elizabethan. The visually striking west side of the house, which is seen from the walk, was remodelled to its present Gothic form, known as Strawberry Hill Gothic, in the 1750s.

Go through the gate, turn left and go through another gate, following the driveway past the converted stable block, and turn right just before the **church**. Follow the path through the churchyard and leave through a gate.

> Inside the **Church of St Mary Magdalene** are memorials to the Hampden family, including those to Richard Hampden (d.1662) and Elizabeth, wife of John Hampden (mentioned earlier). There is also a bas-relief memorial depicting the Civil War Battle of Chalgrove Field (18 June 1643), where John Hampden was fatally wounded.

Continue alongside the fence (right), passing a stand of trees, and go through a gate at the field corner beside a **mound**. ▸ Keep ahead, cross the surfaced track and continue across the field; keep ahead at the path junction, with trees to the right, and go between the houses. Follow the driveway to the left and at the crossroads, with the Hampden Arms just to your left, go straight over and follow the road (Memorial Road) alongside the cricket pitch and back to the start.

The mound is thought to be a medieval motte on which a small keep would have been located.

WALK 17
Great Missenden and Chartridge

Start/finish	Pay and display car park on A4128 in Great Missenden, just south-west off A413 (SP 895 014); or Great Missenden railway station (SP 893 013)
Distance	13.8km (8½ miles) or 10.5km (6½ miles)
Ascent	270m or 175m
Time	4hrs or 3hrs
Map	OS Explorer 181
Refreshments	Pubs, cafés and shops at Great Missenden; The Bell (01494 782878) at Chartridge
Public transport	Train and bus links to Great Missenden

The Chilterns to the west of Chesham consist of several parallel valleys and this undulating walk passes through three of them. The route starts at Great Missenden and heads north-west through Ballinger Common to reach the ridge-top village of Chartridge. From here it crosses back over the valleys, passing the site of a medieval earthwork, before descending past the parish church and following the High Street back through Great Missenden. A shorter walk, missing out Chartridge, is also described.

From the railway station head north to the main road and then right down to a roundabout. Turn right and then left at the next roundabout to reach the car park on the right.

With the car park entrance behind you, head south-south-east along the left edge of the grassy area, following the South Bucks Way. ◄ Keep ahead past houses and a school to reach a green (The Square). Turn left and go through two underpasses (A413 and B485), then head steeply uphill to a lane. Turn left and take the narrow path between the stables (left) and driveway (right), keep ahead through trees and leave through a gate. Turn right, go through another gate and follow the enclosed path uphill, with trees on the left. Continue straight on through two fields, later passing beneath power lines and at the field corner bear half-left through the trees (this route may

GREAT MISSENDEN

The Red Pump Garage on High Street is thought to have been an inspiration for one of Roald Dahl's books

Great Missenden, tucked in the Misbourne Valley – which provided a relatively easy route through the Chilterns between London and the Midlands via Wendover – once had a number of coaching inns along its High Street to cater for the high volume of travellers (it wasn't until 1892 that the railway arrived with the opening of the Metropolitan Line from London Marylebone). Great Missenden is probably best known as the home of the world-famous children's author Roald Dahl (1916–1990), who lived and wrote here for over 30 years. To learn more about the man and his writing, visit the Roald Dahl Museum and Story Centre on the High Street (01494 892192).

Dahl is buried at the Parish Church of St Peter and St Paul, which is passed near the end of the walk. The present building dates from the 14th century, albeit with various additions and alteration over the centuries.

111

be altered when the HS2 rail link is constructed). The earthworks located within the wood are the remains of a medieval manor site.

Continue across the field to a stile in the corner with buildings to the left. Cross the road and go through a gate into the field, where the path splits. Fork left (straight on) for 100m; go through a hedge-gap and follow the right-hand hedge then cross a stile in the east corner. Turn left along the enclosed path as it soon bears right towards **Ballinger Common**. Cross the road and take the gravel driveway ahead (Bull Cottage). At the end, continue along the enclosed path, pass a gate and follow the path for 600m. Just before the track junction turn left (north) through a gate, following the enclosed Chiltern Link for 500m.

Shortcut

Continue eastwards for 25m to a track and turn right; at the right-hand bend go straight on, following a narrow path. Keep ahead down through trees to a road, turn left to the junction and take the bridleway straight on between the two roads to rejoin the walk at SP 923 024; turn right.

At the junction, where the Chiltern Link goes left (west), keep ahead along the enclosed path and turn right into Bellows Wood, where the path splits. Turn left down to the bottom and go right along the bridleway. Take the first left for 75m and turn right (footpath) up through the trees to reach a cross junction. Keep ahead along the enclosed bridleway, with a field to the right, and later bear left. Keep left to follow the track and lane to a T-junction in the peaceful ridge-top village of **Chartridge**. Turn right past the village hall, and once level with The Bell pub turn right through the bushes and a gate. Head half-right across the field, continue along the right-hand edge to cross a stile at the corner, and follow the enclosed path as it goes left to cross another stile. Turn right alongside the right-hand field hedge and then go down through the trees (steps). Cross the road, then a stile and follow the right-hand boundary up through two fields. Continue straight on through the middle of a third field, go through a gate and turn left to a road at **Little Pednor Farm**.

Take a short 50m detour left to see the picturesque **Pednor House** (beside Little Pednor Farm), which dates from the 17th century. The unusual cylindrical brick dovecote in the centre of the courtyard was built in 1910.

The dovecote at Pednor House

The 12th- or 13th-century earthworks, like those passed earlier, are the remains of a former manor site with moat which at one time belonged to Missenden Abbey.

Cross over and follow the enclosed path; continue through the trees and then go steeply down across the field to a crossing bridleway (SP 923 024 – the point at which the shortcut rejoins the main route). Keep ahead up through the trees to a lane and turn left for a few metres and then right along the driveway for Reddings Farm. After 150m turn right and follow the hedge on the left as it soon turns left to pass the farm, continue for 250m and then turn left over a stile. Follow the enclosed path, cross a stile and at the fild corner turn right along the field edge for 100m. Bear half-left through the beech trees, heading south-west past old **earthworks** (there are several paths within the open access wood) to reach a junction on the western edge. ◄

Bear left (south), staying within the wood, and then keep ahead along the gravel path to a surfaced lane. Go right for 100m and then left along the enclosed path;

keep ahead through three fields to a road (B485) opposite Hyde Lane. Cross over and turn left, and just after the driveway turn right through the trees and gate.

Follow the right-hand field boundary, pass into the next field and bear right. Cross a stile and head diagonally left to a cross path in the dip, turn right heading south-west downhill, keeping right of the trees; cross another stile and bear right, following the track up to a minor road beside **Hyde Farm**. Turn right for 100m past Chapel Farm and turn left into the trees, continuing past a building and enter a field, where the path splits. Turn left, following the left-hand edge, continue through the second field for 250m then pass into a third field and follow the right-hand hedge. Pass under the power lines to the corner and keep ahead through the next field. Cross a hedge-lined track to the right of **Rook Wood** and continue downhill, keeping on the right-hand side of the valley. Turn right through a gate to enter the churchyard and bear left to pass around the **church**.

Heading back down to Great Missenden near Rook Wood

The Parish Church of St Peter and St Paul

Turn left along the drive towards **Great Missenden**, cross the bridge (A413) and follow the lane down to a junction. Keep left along Church Street then right along the High Street, passing the Roald Dahl Museum (right) and then the old Red Pump Garage – a fictionalised version of which is said to feature in Dahl's book *Danny, the Champion of the World* – to reach a roundabout. Turn right (A4128) to go back to the **car park**. (For the railway station keep ahead, turn left at the next roundabout and continue to the station entrance.)

4 AMERSHAM TO HIGH WYCOMBE

Heading east through the aptly named Walk Wood towards Chenies (Walk 18)

WALK 18

Chenies, Latimer and the River Chess

Start/finish	Roadside parking on Stony Lane (road to Latimer), 350m south of the A404 (TQ 004 982)
Alternative start	Chalfont and Latimer railway station (SU 996 975)
Distance	8.8km (5½ miles) or 10.3km (6½ miles)
Ascent	150m or 160m
Time	2½hrs or 3hrs
Maps	OS Explorer 172
Refreshments	Bedford Arms (01923 283301) and Red Lion (01923 282722) at Chenies
Public transport	Bus links from junction of Stony Lane and A404 (detour) to Watford and High Wycombe; trains to Chalfont and Latimer station (detour)

An easy half-day walk exploring a peaceful section of the beautiful Chess Valley just to the north of Chorleywood. The first half of the route follows the south side of the valley, passing through picturesque Chenies before crossing the River Chess – one of the jewels of the Chilterns. The return section follows the north side of the valley, passing watercress beds and a nature reserve and visiting picture-postcard Latimer. After crossing the river again the route heads back to the start.

Alternative start: Chalfont and Latimer railway station

Head east along Amersham Road (A404) and go left along Chessfield Park to a right-hand bend. Go straight on between houses and continue past the recreation ground into the trees. Turn right, joining the main route at TQ 000 981. Follow the bridleway eastwards to reach a road, then turn right and continue to the parking area.

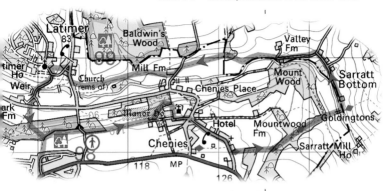

From the parking area head east across the road to enter
Walk Wood and follow the bridleway straight ahead for
700m. At the split go straight on through a gate into the
trees; at the first junction fork left and then go straight
on (level path) at the cross junction. At the far woodland
boundary turn right (uphill), continue between brick
walls to a drive with the **Manor House** to the right, and
turn left down past the **church**.

> **Chenies** was known as 'Isenhampstead' until the
> mid-13th century when the Cheyne family took
> over the **manor**. The manor house remained with
> the family until the 16th century when it passed by
> marriage to John Russell, later 1st Earl of Bedford,
> and remained with the Russell family until the
> 1950s (opening times: 01494 762888). The adja-
> cent 15th-century St Michael's Church houses a
> fine collection of memorials to members of the
> Russell family in the Bedford Chapel, described by
> the architectural historian Nikolaus Pevsner as 'the
> richest single storehouse of funeral monuments in
> any parish church in England'. The chapel is not
> open to the public but can be viewed through the
> windows.

*The colourful
village sign*

119

The Red Lion in Chenies

Keep ahead between the two halves of the village green – to the right is the old well – and continue straight on (south-east) along the road for Chorleywood for 550m, soon passing the Bedford Arms and later the Red Lion (pavement on right). After the last house on the left, turn left across the road and go through two gates (house on left), following the enclosed Chiltern Way and soon heading down through Wyburn Wood. Continue across the field and bear left alongside Turveylane Wood, soon doglegging right to continue down through the trees. Go through a gate and keep ahead at the cross-path junction through the meadow and cross the **River Chess** to reach a path junction.

Turn left through the gate and follow the track northwards to join a lane at a corner in **Sarratt Bottom**. Go straight on along the lane, and at the right-hand bend turn left on a track and continue for 400m to reach a junction. To the left is the watercress farm and a footbridge across the river, while sharp right goes to **Valley Farm**; we go straight on along the enclosed path (wooden walkway) between these routes, following the Chess Valley Way. ◀

Information boards give details about water voles and the Frogmore Meadow Nature Reserve.

Continue through Limeshill Wood to a gate, then go through a field and gate and follow an enclosed path to a lane. Turn left, and just before the bridge go right along a gravel drive at Mill Farm Barns. Dogleg left through a gate and continue along the enclosed route. Keep ahead at the junction and shortly pass the tomb of William Liberty (d.1777), then go through a gate. To the left are the ruins of a **church**.

> An information board details the history of the 13th-century St Mary Magdalene Church (no access). **William Liberty**, related to the founders of the famous Liberty's store in London, asked to be buried here alone so that he could identify his bones after he was resurrected.

Keep to the right-hand boundary, and where the fence turns right go straight on to a road and turn right to the green in **Latimer** (to the left is the River Chess).

The footbridge over the River Chess on the way past Sarratt Bottom

The village green in **Latimer**, with its old water pump and memorials to local men who fought in the Boer War – and to a horse that was injured at the Battle of Boshof in South Africa – is surrounded by picturesque 17th- and 18th-century cottages. The red-brick 19th-century Church of St Mary Magdelane was built by Sir George Gilbert Scott; beyond is the rather imposing Victorian Latimer House (now a hotel), which replaced the original Elizabethan structure.

Turn left (green on right) and go straight across at the next road junction to follow a path between the houses. Cross the driveway, go through a gate and head across the field, just right of some pine trees, to reach a gate. Continue through the trees to the road and turn left. (To visit the church, turn right and then left along the driveway with Latimer House beyond.)

Follow the road down to a bend and take the second entrance on the right, passing a gate and heading downhill with **Latimer House** to the right. Cross the River Chess with a **weir** to the right and continue straight on across the field.

Cross the road, go through a gate and fork left alongside the fence up to another gate. Fork left up through West Wood to reach a junction near the top edge (TQ 000 981; to return to the railway station go straight on and retrace the outward route). Stay in the trees and turn left (east) along the bridleway to reach a road. Turn right and go back to the parking area.

WALK 19
Little Missenden, Penn Wood and Penn Street

Start/finish	Roadside parking along minor road for Shardeloes, just off the A413 roundabout to the north-west of Amersham Old Town (SU 947 978); or bus stop on the A404 near Penn Street (SU 923 966) if using public transport
Distance	12.1km (7½ miles) or 8.4km (5¼ miles)
Ascent	165m or 130m
Time	3½hrs or 2½hrs
Map	OS Explorer 172
Refreshments	Crown Inn (01494 862571) and Red Lion (01494 862876) at Little Missenden; The Squirrel (01494 711291) and Hit or Miss (01494 713109) at Penn Street
Public transport	Daily bus links to the A404 at Penn Street from Chesham and High Wycombe

The walk heads north-west along the Misbourne Valley, overlooked by the imposing outline of Shardeloes House, to arrive at the scenic village of Little Missenden – home to a couple of pubs and a church with some stunning 13th-century wall paintings. From here the route sets off to explore the ancient woodland of Penn Wood before calling in at Penn Street and heading back to the Misbourne Valley. A shorter option, missing out Penn Street, is also described.

Head south-east along the minor road and turn right through the gated entrance for Shardeloes House. Immediately fork right along the South Bucks Way and continue past the cricket pavilion, leaving through a gate in the far fence. Follow the enclosed path, going through a gate and keeping ahead with the **lake** on the right and Shardeloes House up to the left. ▶

> **Shardeloes House** was built for William Drake, MP for Amersham for 50 years, in the second half of the 18th century. A grand, white neoclassical mansion,

The lake forms part of the River Misbourne, which rises just north of Great Missenden and flows south through the Misbourne Valley to join the River Colne near Denham.

Following the South Bucks Way towards Little Missenden

it was designed by Stiff Leadbetter, although it was completed and improved by Robert Adam. The building, which became a maternity hospital during WWII, was later saved from demolition and converted into private apartments.

Go through a gate slightly left of the field corner and keep ahead, later passing through two gates either side of a crossing bridleway. Continue along the left-hand hedge and then along the track. Bear left on the road through **Little Missenden**, passing the Crown Inn, then Missenden House (starred as Dibley Manor in *The Vicar of Dibley* TV series) and later the Red Lion pub, and keep left (straight on) at the junction with Taylors Lane. At the next junction the walk goes left along the road for Holmer Green. (To visit the church go straight on for 50m, afterwards retracing your steps and turning right.)

Little Missenden is home to the ancient Church of St John the Baptist, which dates back to Saxon times with various additions and alterations through to the 15th century. Consider paying a visit to see some lovely 13th-century wall paintings, including one of St Christopher and, to the right of this, a series depicting scenes from the life of St Catherine. There are also several colourful Victorian stained glass windows.

Some may recognise parts of the village due to its starring role in a number of film and TV productions, including several episodes of *Midsomer Murders*.

Follow the road southwards to a sharp right-hand bend, fork left past a gate and head south-west diagonally up across the field. Go through a gate and turn right along the bridleway (Toby's Lane) for 2km.

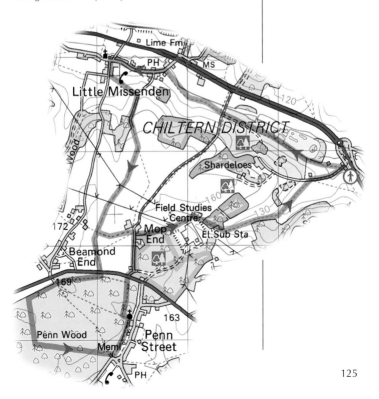

Shortcut
Some 350m after passing the second set of powerlines, turn left at the first crossing path (SU 919 971) and go across the field; go through the hedge and turn left, following the hedge eastwards, then cross the lane and take the path opposite, rejoining the main walk (SU 924 971).

With care, cross the road (A404) and go through a gate opposite to enter **Penn Wood**.

> Until the Enclosure Acts of the mid-19th century, **Penn Wood** was part of Wycombe Heath, an area of common land where locals could graze their livestock. Wood from the forest was also used in a thriving furniture industry, including that of bodgers, who made chair legs and spindles.

The tree was presented by HRH Prince Charles to commemorate the Woodland Trust's successful fight to save Penn Wood from development in 1999.

Keep ahead for 50m to a crossing path and turn right, following a path parallel with the road. Keep ahead at the next crossing path for 200m to reach Beamond End Pond (the right of way goes left and then takes the right-hand fork through a gate before keeping left through the wood to reach the road at **Penn Street**). Continue for a further 175m before swinging left (southwards) for 400m to reach a crossing path (grassy ride). Turn left for 675m, keeping ahead at a crossing path beside a copper beech. ◀

Later follow the path as it bears left to reach a crossing track (this is the official right of way). Turn right to a road at **Penn Street** and go left, following a path alongside the trees with the large grassy Penn Common and The Squirrel pub over to the right (the Hit or Miss pub is a short way south-east along the road for Winchmore Hill and Amersham, opposite the cricket ground). Pass to the left of the **war memorial** and pond to reach a parking area, then keep ahead to the **church**.

> The small village of **Penn Street** lies along the road between Amersham and Penn, overlooking the large green and cricket pitch. Holy Trinity Church, with its tall, striking spire, was built in 1849.

Holy Trinity Church in Penn Street

Just before the churchyard gate, turn left for 100m then turn right and head northwards for 400m. Where the main path swings left, keep right (straight on) and shortly leave the wood through a gate to arrive at a bus stop (SU 923 966). With care, cross over the road, turn left to the junction and go right for 50m before turning left across the road and following the lane towards **Mop End**.

Shortly after some houses on the right, turn right on a crossing path (SU 924 971 – the point at which the short-cut rejoins). Follow the path parallel to the woodland edge before bearing left past a metal pylon; to the right is a large **electricity substation** (hidden by trees). Follow the path as it bears right under power lines and heads gently down through the trees, ignoring any side paths. Bear left into a field and follow the right-hand hedge, ignoring a crossing track and following a line of trees and bushes on the right towards Lower Park House. Go through the gate and turn right down the drive, passing the cricket pitch and gated entrance, to arrive back at the start point.

WALK 20

Hughenden, Bradenham and West Wycombe

Start/finish	Car park beside Hughenden Church (SU 864 955), 2.4km north of High Wycombe on the A4128
Distance	13km (8 miles)
Ascent	395m
Time	4hrs
Maps	OS Explorer 172
Refreshments	Café at Hughenden Manor; Red Lion Tea Room (01494 565554) at Bradenham; shop, café and several pubs at West Wycombe; Le De Spencers Arms (01494 535317) at Downley
Public transport	Bus links to Hughenden Manor entrance (A4128) from High Wycombe and Aylesbury

This walk, exploring the area around three stately homes, starts from Hughenden and passes over wooded Naphill Common before visiting Bradenham with its pretty cottages, manor and church overlooking the village green. After passing over West Wycombe Hill, crowned by St Lawrence's Church and the Dashwood Mausoleum, the walk heads through West Wycombe and back to Hughenden. Along the way you can visit Hughenden Manor, West Wycombe House (detour) or the Hellfire Caves.

Views to the left include the D'Israeli Monument, commemorating Benjamin's father, Isaac.

From the church follow the drive uphill past the café and walled garden (right) and **Hughenden Manor** (left). Once over the brow of the hill, follow the track down through the trees for 100m and fork right at the marker post (signposted to Naphill), soon following a path with Hanging Wood on the right. ◄ Once back in the trees turn left at the junction heading downhill and then right along the wooded valley for 600m, go through a gate and keep ahead through the field. Turn left along the lane to a bend at **Hunt's Hill** where there is a map of Naphill Common (numerous routes across the open access common can make route-finding difficult).

HUGHENDEN MANOR

Hughenden Manor was the country hideaway of the Victorian Prime Minister and author Benjamin Disraeli (1804–1881), who spent his childhood at nearby Bradenham Manor and then lived at Hughenden from 1848 until his death. During WWII the manor was used as a secret intelligence base, code-named 'Hillside', where Air Ministry staff analysed aerial photographs of Germany and created maps for bombing missions (National Trust: 01494 755565). The nearby Church of St Michael and All Angels dates from the 12th century but underwent extensive Victorian restorations. Outside, at the eastern end of the church, is the Disraeli tomb – resting place of Disraeli and his wife, Mary Anne.

Turn right, following the track as it soon curves left, and after the power line turn right and follow a bridleway north-north-west through the trees of **Naphill Common** for 600m to reach a bridleway junction at SU 843 968. To your right (through the trees) is **Naphill**. Turn left (west), follow the bridleway for 1km and keep ahead along the track, passing a cottage and then starting to descend.

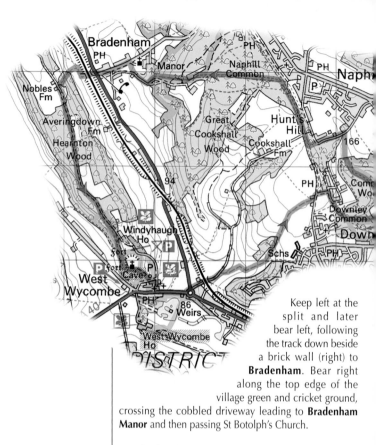

Keep left at the split and later bear left, following the track down beside a brick wall (right) to **Bradenham**. Bear right along the top edge of the village green and cricket ground, crossing the cobbled driveway leading to **Bradenham Manor** and then passing St Botolph's Church.

The brick-built **Bradenham Manor** dates from 1670 and was once the home of Isaac D'Israeli (1766–1848). His son, Benjamin, used Bradenham Manor as the inspiration for Hurstley in his novel *Endymion*. The adjacent St Botolph's Church dates from the 12th century.

Turn left down the road and go past some lovely cottages to reach a T-junction with the A4010. On the right is the Red Lion tea room. Turn right for 50m and then left, carefully crossing the road, and go through the gate (bus stop to the right). Head south-west across the narrow field, pass under the railway bridge and dogleg left to follow the right-hand field edge. Shortly turn right through a gate, follow the left-hand hedge for 100m and go left through another gate where the path splits. Keep left, following the path up the left side of the field and continue up through the trees to a drive at **Nobles Farm**.

Turn left (the walk now follows this ridge-top track for 1.8km towards West Wycombe), passing through a gate and ignoring all crossing routes. Much later, pass near **Windyhaugh House** and continue through the car park, keeping to the right-hand side and aiming for the church. Go through the gate and follow the path past the church, staying right of the wall, to reach the Dashwood Mausoleum on West Wycombe Hill.

Perched high above West Wycombe, on the site of an Iron Age hill fort, **St Lawrence's Church** is easily recognisable by its 'Golden Ball' crowning the tower. If it's open, take a look inside to see a striking painting of The Last Supper by Giovanni Borgnis, and for a small charge you can climb the tower for a great view. The adjacent Dashwood Mausoleum was built in 1765.

Head south-east down the grassy slope for 200m. In the distance is the straight-running A40 leading out of West Wycombe; soon there are views of **West Wycombe House** to the right. Turn right down the second set of steps to pass the Hellfire Caves and café (01494 533739). ▶

Turn left along the road, then sharp right down Church Lane and pass through the archway of the 15th-century brick and timber Church Loft – once a pilgrim's rest house. To the right from here is the George and Dragon Hotel, The Plough and The Swan Inn, and slightly further on is the entrance to West Wycombe House.

The caves were extended by Sir Francis Dashwood in the 1740s – a winding underground passage leads you through the Banqueting Hall and Inner Temple.

Allow time for a visit to West Wycombe House and park

The 18th-century Italianate **West Wycombe House**, rebuilt by Sir Francis Dashwood – who became Lord Despencer and is probably best remembered for his infamous Hellfire Club – has been the home of the Dashwood family for over 300 years. The surrounding parkland, which features several follies, was landscaped by Humphry Repton. (National Trust: 01494 755571.)

Turn left (east) along the High Street (A40), passing the shop, and at the roundabout circle clockwise across Bradenham Road and follow Cookshall Lane with the garage on the right. Go under the railway bridge and after 150m fork right along a bridleway beside the right-hand hedge. Start climbing and after 600m fork left, still following the sunken way uphill to reach a lane at **Downley** with the cricket pitch opposite. Turn left and follow the lane as it bends right to a T-junction and houses (125m to the left is the Le De Spencers Arms).

Turn right along the track (houses on left) to the left bend and go straight on across the open grassy area. Continue down through the trees to a five-way junction in a dip. Turn left (bridleway) down the valley, ignore a crossing path and keep ahead along the enclosed track. Enter the woods and follow the main track slightly left and then uphill, ignoring all crossing routes, to reach the drive at **Hughenden Manor**. Head back down to the church.

WALK 21
Penn and Coleshill

Start/finish	Widmer Pond, beside the B474 at Penn and Tylers Green (SU 907 937); limited roadside parking
Distance	13km (8 miles) or 6.9km (4¼ miles)
Ascent	255m or 160m
Time	3¾hrs or 2hrs
Maps	OS Explorer 172
Refreshments	Red Lion (01494 813107), The Crown (01494 812640) and village shop at Penn; Potters Arms (01494 726222), The Plough (01494 259757) and village shop at Winchmore Hill; Red Lion (01494 723718) at Coleshill
Public transport	Daily bus services to Penn from High Wycombe and Beaconsfield

This walk, situated between Beaconsfield and Amersham, meanders through a patchwork of woods and open fields. From Penn, with its attractive village pond, the walk heads east through Winchmore Hill to reach Coleshill – and another lovely pond – before heading back. A shortcut, effectively splitting the route in two, is also described.

The village of **Penn** lies adjacent to its neighbour, Tylers Green, and has a history stretching back many centuries. By the 12th century the manor was held by the de la Penne family, who remained until the death of Roger Penn (d.1731), the last male heir. The manor then passed by marriage to the Curzon family; they in turn took the title of Earl Howe and the estate is now held by the 7th Earl Howe.

At one time the village was noted for producing floor tiles using local clay deposits.

From the pond (Widmer Pond) cross the B474 and take the track just left of the Red Lion pub to **Puttenham Place Farm**. Follow the track, keeping right of the buildings, to

The sign at Tylers Green does the village justice

enter a field, then turn left alongside the hedge to reach a path junction. Stay in the same field and turn right, following the left-hand hedge through the next field. At a path junction, 75m after the start of Brook Wood (left), go left into the trees.

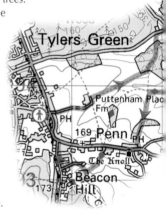

Keep ahead at the junction and head down through the trees. Continue across the field and turn right down the road to a T-junction.

Cross over and follow the fence up to a track, turn left for 10m and then right (marker post) up through the trees of Pennhouse Grove.

Heading towards Winchmore Hill

Keep ahead across the field, go through a hedge-gap and cross the tree-lined drive that leads to **Penn House**. Go through the gate opposite and head half-right across the field to leave through another gate.

Shortcut

Turn sharp right and follow the Chiltern Way for 700m through the trees, rejoining the main walk at SU 925 942.

Cross Horsemoor Lane, pass the pond and go through a gate. (The walk now follows the Chiltern Way for 2.8km.) Continue between fences to **Winchmore Hill**, pass a gate and bear half-right across the common to a skewed crossroads; to the right is the Potters Arms pub. Take the second left (The Hill) towards Amersham, with The Plough on your right, and once level with the Primitive Methodist Chapel (left) turn right between the houses.

Follow the right-hand hedge through two fields, passing under the power lines. Keep ahead through the trees and then across the field, passing just right of a copse. Go through a gate and head eastwards alongside the trees, later following the driveway past Lands Farm in **Coleshill**. Cross the road and follow the enclosed path past the church to another road. To your right (25m) is the picturesque village pond and a seat.

The pond at Coleshill

Coleshill, noted as the birthplace of the English poet and politician Edmund Waller (1606–1687), is home to the Victorian All Saints Church, designed by the Neo-Gothic architect George Street. The rare starfruit marsh plant (*Damasonium alisma*) has been found growing in the village pond.

Cross the road and head along the left side of the car park, passing the Red Lion pub. Continue downhill to a field and bear right then left along the field boundary to reach a cross-path junction. Turn right (leaving the Chiltern Way) and follow the grassy strip between fields to a path junction. Continue straight across the next field, go through a gate and follow the right-hand field edge to a road by the entrance to **Bowers Farm**.

Cross over slightly leftwards, go through a gate and keep ahead into a field. Turn right then left alongside a line of trees, heading towards **Ongar Hill Farm**. Turn right along the track to a junction and head south-west (slightly left) over the grassy area to reach another track.

Keep ahead (west), following the field edge on the right; 150m after passing under the power lines bear right down through the trees into a field and cross-junction. Turn right along the field edge, ignore the first gate on the right and shortly go through the next gate. Head north-west across the field with **Luckings Farm** to the right; go through a gate and then straight on down the enclosed path.

Dogleg right and continue up beside the field edge, stay in the field and turn right, then continue along the minor road to reach a junction beside a house. Go left (Coleshill Lane) for a few metres, and just after the house turn left through a gate and follow the left-hand field edge. Go through another gate and turn right along the road (Fagnall Lane), passing Lowlands and the entrance to **Glory Farm**, and just before Fagnall Farm (right) turn sharp left through a gate and head south across the field towards the buildings. Go through a gate and turn right to the top right corner. Pass through two gates, cross the track and follow the right-hand hedge, later passing through the hedge, and continue with the hedge on the left. Cross the lane (Horsemoor Lane) and head half-left across the field, then continue downhill just inside Branches Wood. Cross the drive and continue to a junction with the Chiltern Way (SU 925 942 – the shortcut rejoins the main route here).

Bear left (Chiltern Way) to leave the trees and stay in the left–hand field, following the right-hand margin downhill, and curve right to pass a gate. Cross the road and go through the gate opposite before turning right, following the permissive path alongside the hedge, and soon turn right again through another gate. Cross the minor road and take the track opposite (parking area) at **Penn Bottom**.

Keep left (straight on), following the track (Chiltern Way) along the valley for 300m, to reach a crossing path. Turn left up the grassy strip across the field. Keep ahead through the trees and follow the path alongside the car park; once past the hedge turn right and then bear right along the road (B474) through **Penn** for 400m, passing

The 12th-century Holy Trinity Church at Penn

The Crown pub (right) and the 12th-century Holy Trinity Church (left).

Call into the **church** to see the rare 15th-century painting of the Last Judgement (or 'Doom') on wooden panels hanging above the chancel arch, while in the family vault lie the remains of six grandchildren of William Penn, the Quaker and founder of Pennsylvania. The churchyard is the final resting place of the Russian spy, Donald Maclean, who defected in 1951.

At Wellbank (house) turn left across the road and follow the Chiltern Way between the houses to a T-junction in the trees. Turn right along the bridleway for 100m, then turn left along the drive to a lane at **Beacon Hill**. Turn right along the lane for 300m, cross the road (B474) and turn left. Soon fork right along Elm Road to arrive back at the pond.

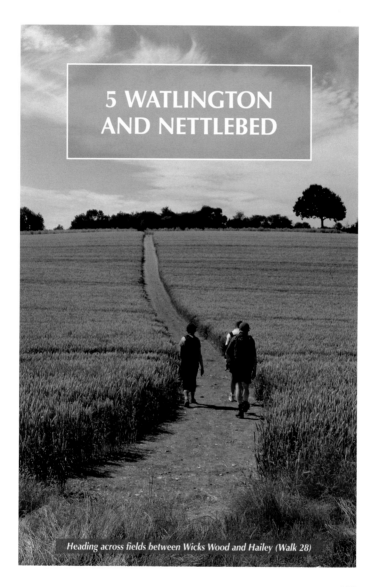

5 WATLINGTON
AND NETTLEBED

Heading across fields between Wicks Wood and Hailey (Walk 28)

WALK 22

Christmas Common and Watlington Hill

Start/finish	Cowleaze Wood car park (SU 725 956), between Christmas Common and Stokenchurch
Distance	13.3km (8¼ miles)
Ascent	410m
Time	4hrs
Maps	OS Explorer 171
Refreshments	Fox and Hounds (01491 612599) at Christmas Common; Carriers Arms (01491 613470), Fat Fox Inn (01491 613040), The Chequers (01491 612874) and shops at Watlington (detour)
Public transport	Watlington (detour) has bus links to Oxford

From Cowleaze Wood the walk heads through an undulating landscape of beech woods and open countryside, passing close to Wormsley Park to reach Christmas Common. From here it's off to Watlington Hill for a great view before heading up Shirburn Hill and back to Cowleaze Wood. Take in a detour to Watlington or, once you've finished the walk, explore the adjacent Aston Rowant National Nature Reserve (access opposite the car park entrance).

At Cowleaze Wood stand with your back to the car park entrance and take the wide path south-east past the vehicle barrier. Cross the grass ride and continue through the trees, ignoring a path to the right and soon heading eastwards. ◄

Some 250m after the grass ride and 50m to the left of the path is a memorial to the crew of a WWII Halifax bomber that crashed here in 1944 (SU 729 955).

Keep to the main path, heading east; leave through a gate and continue down across two fields. Turn left along the surfaced drive for 50m and then right through a gate, heading down beside a hedge at **Lower Vicar's Farm**. Follow the hedge to the left and turn right through another gate. Head half-left up across the field and continue up through **Hailey Wood**, heading generally north-north-east to a crossing track (bridleway). Turn right along

Looking back along the route, having passed Wormsley Park

this and go downhill, later heading more steeply down towards **Wellground Farm**. Turn right along the surfaced drive, passing left of a thatched cottage, keep left (straight on) at the junction and continue for 400m. ▶ Where the drive turns right (private), continue straight on along the track for 250m to an open field and continue alongside the left-hand fence for 225m.

At the junction fork right, following the level bridleway between the fence (left) and trees (right) and continue for 600m to reach a junction with the Chiltern Way. Turn right through the gate and head west across two fields separated by a surfaced track with gates. Leave the second field through a gate and bear right along the drive for 25m before forking left, soon with a brick and flint wall on the right. Fork right at the split; cross a track and continue straight on past a large stone urn to follow a wide path through the trees for 1.7km, heading generally westwards.

Continue through **Blackmoor Wood**, ignoring a path off to the left, and later head more steeply up through

To the right through the trees you might just see the white-painted Wormsley Park, an 18th-century house that was once the home of the philanthropist Sir Paul Getty (1932–2003).

141

Shotridge Wood to a junction near the top edge of the wood. Bear right for 75m, passing just right of some disused pits, to a path junction and turn left, passing through an old boundary bank and ditch. Continue south-westwards for 200m (look for the white arrows on the trees) to join a track. Turn left to pass Magpie Cottage, then go right at the junction and follow the enclosed path as it curves left to the road at **Christmas Common**. (To visit The Fox and Hounds pub go left along the road to a split and then fork right for 100m.)

Follow the road to the right, then go left at the junction for 400m before turning left into **Watlington Hill car park** (not the waymarked path). Take the first path on the right past the information boards, heading through the trees. Cross a track and soon go through a gate to follow the broad grassy strip westwards along Watlington Hill past some seats (left). To the right, and later ahead, are some great views. ◀ Keep to the grassy strip between bushes and bear half-right (north-west), soon descending steeply past the **White Mark** to a gate.

The view north follows the Chiltern scarp to Beacon Hill and Aston Rowant National Nature Reserve, while to the north-west is Watlington.

The **White Mark**, an 82m-long 'obelisk', was cut into the chalk by Edward Horne in 1764. It is said he felt the parish church

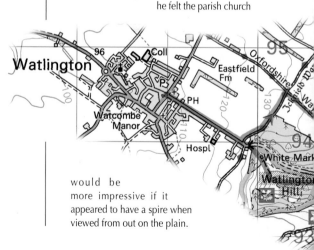

would be more impressive if it appeared to have a spire when viewed from out on the plain.

Keep ahead and later bear left down Hill Road for a few metres to the junction with the Ridgeway (track). Turn right across the road.

Detour to Watlington

Follow Hill Road and continue past the Carriers Arms to the High Street; The Fat Fox Inn and The Chequers are both to the right. Retrace your steps back to the main route (2km return).

Watlington is reputedly England's smallest town, although it no longer holds a market. In the centre, surrounded by historic buildings, is the Town

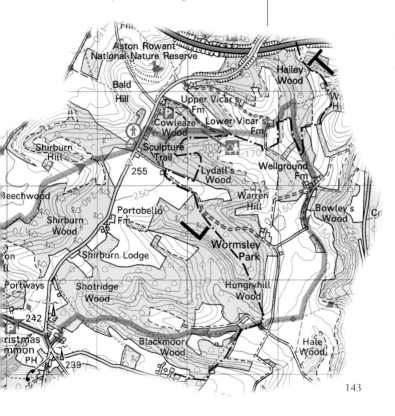

Looking north-west over Watlington from the White Mark on Watlington Hill

Hall, built by Thomas Stonor in 1665. North-west of the centre is St Leonard's Church, which contains a sculpture of St Leonard – a sixth century French monk – by local resident Faith Tolkien; he is also portrayed in the west window.

Follow the Ridgeway north-eastwards for 750m to a lane and turn right, following the Oxfordshire Way for 400m. Turn left through a gate and head through the scrub, soon following the left-hand fence with **Pyrton Hill** to the right. Go through a gate and continue alongside **Shirburn Wood** with a field to the left; turn right at the end and follow the fence along two sides of the field with trees to the right, later heading through the bushes to a gate. Head north-eastwards up **Shirburn Hill** (this area of open access land is home to distinctive juniper scrub) – looking back for a great view – then go through a gate and keep ahead to cross a track and stile. Continue across the field, aiming for the house, and cross a stile in the corner. Turn left along the road and just after the water tower follow a parallel path on the right just in the trees back to the **car park**. ◄

On the left side of the road is Aston Rowant National Nature Reserve which contains a mix of species-rich chalk grassland and woodland.

WALK 23

Turville, Skirmett and Fingest

Start/finish	Village green in Turville (SU 767 911); limited roadside parking
Distance	11.3km (7 miles) or 5.5km (3½ miles)
Ascent	480m or 230m
Time	3¾hrs or 1¾hrs
Maps	OS Explorer 171
Refreshments	Bull and Butcher (01491 638283) at Turville; The Frog (01491 638996) at Skirmett; Chequers Inn (01491 638335) at Fingest
Public transport	None

A hilly route offering some great views across the upper reaches of the Hambleden Valley. From Turville, overlooked by a handsome windmill, the route climbs up to Ibstone and then meanders through scenic countryside to visit Skirmett and Fingest, home to a rare twin-gabled church tower, before arriving back at Turville. A shorter walk, missing out Ibstone, is also described.

TURVILLE

Cottages at Turville, overlooked by Cobstone Windmill

This picture-postcard village, which starred in the BBC TV series *The Vicar of Dibley* and several of ITV's *Midsomer Murders*, has a fine collection of 16th- to 18th-century cottages, as well as the inviting timber-framed Bull and Butcher pub. The 12th-century flint church of St Mary the Virgin boasts a few Norman features, though most of what you see is around 700 years old. A more recent addition is the beautiful stained glass window by John Piper, who spent much of his working life at Fawley Bottom near Henley-on-Thames.

Shorter option
From the village green head south along School Lane and gently up past cottages and the school. Continue along the bridleway, pass through a gate and follow the right-hand field edge straight on. The longer walk shortly joins through a gate on the right (SU 765 908); follow the main route description from this point.

From the village green in Turville follow the road north-westwards for 150m, passing the church. Once level with The Old Vicarage, turn right on a path between houses. Head half-left across the field, go through two gates in the top-left corner and continue for a few metres before turning left through another gate. Follow the path up through the trees and scrub for 175m to a gate.

Continue up beside the fence (left), go through a gate and turn left alongside the fence with trees on your right for 300m, ignoring a path to the right. At the fence corner go right for a few metres and then left, heading north-west for 150m through Park Wood. Fork right at the marker post and follow a narrow path north-north-west through the trees, keeping a lookout for another marker post where the path bears right (north) up to the road close to **Ibstone House**. ▸

The 18th-century house was once owned by the famed author Dame Rebecca West.

Turn left to a road junction and go left (west), following a waymarked path over a stile beside the gate (not the road); go along the right-hand fence before keeping straight on into the trees for 25m to a junction. Turn left (south) for 300m, and once level with the small, mainly Norman, Church of St Nicholas (left), turn right down to a stile and then left along the upper field boundary, later following it down through a gate. Keep ahead through another gate and bear right through Turville Wood.

Cross the farm track and keep ahead – a bridleway joins from the left – and in 50m fork left to a road beside an entrance to Wormsley Estate. Cross the road and stile before following the right-hand fence; continue up through the trees and turn left along the track through Idlecombe Wood for 1km. At the T-junction turn up to the right through Churchfield Wood, ignoring a bridleway and path off to the left, to leave the trees and join a track at **Turville Court**.

Turn left through a gate and follow the enclosed track, continue through a gate and follow the right-hand field edge. Go through another gate and follow the left-hand boundary for 150m to a seat and bear slightly right past the wooden electricity pole, heading downhill with a view of Cobstone Mill. Go through the gate (SU 765 908 – the point at which the shorter walk joins the main route) and turn right alongside the hedge for 75m before forking half-left over the field. Cross the road and take the track opposite through the trees to a field where the path splits; take the left fork (straight on) and soon enter Poynatts Wood. Keep ahead for 25m and then turn left for 300m, following the path as it bends left downhill and then right along the edge of the wood. Turn left, leaving the trees, and follow the enclosed path down towards Skirmett. Follow the track past **Poynatts Farm** to a road and turn right for 125m.

Just before The Frog pub at **Skirmett**, turn left on a track past the village hall. Where this bends right to a house, go straight on through a gate and fork left (straight on) between fences. Go through a gate, cross the field and go through another gate. Turn left up the track and keep ahead to enter Adam's Wood. ◄ Keep to the main path uphill for 500m and at the split fork left (Chiltern Way), still climbing. Leave the wood, turn left and pass a gate to enter a field.

Head slightly right across the field and follow a path down through Fingest Wood. Cross Fieldfare Stile and, after admiring the view, follow the left-hand edge through two fields down towards **Fingest**. ◄ Turn left along the road and keep ahead past The Chequers pub (left) with the church to the right.

Owned by the Woodland Trust, this is a great place for bluebells.

The stile was erected in memory of author Henry Bridges Fearon (1907–1995), who, as 'Fieldfare', brought the joy of the English countryside to many.

The view east across Skirmett and the Hambleden Valley

St Bartholomew's Church in Fingest with its rare twin-gabled tower

Fingest, once home to Sir William Connor (1909–67), who wrote for the Daily Mirror under the name of 'Cassandra', has some delightful cottages, a church and a pub. St Bartholomew's Church (named after one of the 12 apostles) has a very unusual twin-gabled square Norman tower – there may only be one other example in the country – and a painted plaster exterior (most local churches have bare flint).

Just after the churchyard, fork right through a gate and follow an enclosed path (Chiltern Way) to a path junction. Go left, cross the lane and continue beside the fence, skirting round the side of **Turville Hill**. Go through a gate and descend half-left across the field to the far left corner. Up to the right is a **windmill**.

Cobstone Mill (private) is a great example of an 18th-century **smock mill** – the top section of which was designed to revolve so that the sails could be brought in line with the wind. The windmill played a starring role in the film *Chitty Chitty Bang Bang* (written by *James Bond* creator Ian Fleming) as the home of the eccentric inventor Caractacus Potts.

Turn left, going through two gates and follow the track between houses back to the village green in **Turville**, with the pub on the left.

WALK 24
Pishill and Stonor

Start/finish	Car park beside Pishill Church (SU 726 898), off the B480 just north of Stonor
Distance	9.5km (6 miles)
Ascent	320m
Time	3hrs
Maps	OS Explorer 171
Refreshments	Crown Inn (01491 638364) at Pishill (short detour)
Public transport	None

An undulating half-day walk to the north of Henley-on-Thames, offering some lovely views. Call in at the little church in Pishill before heading to Maidensgrove and then dropping down to Stonor. The route then passes through Stonor Park, with a view of historic Stonor House, before heading across the wooded Summer Heath and finally back to Pishill with views to the west.

The small hamlet of Pishill consists of a **church**, a pub and a few houses. The church dates back to Norman times, though it was partially rebuilt in the mid-19th century. Inside there are several interesting stained glass windows, including one by John Piper in memory of Philip Hall that shows St Paul's emblems of the sword and gospel. The gospel is held by two hands in front of the sword, signifying that the pen is mightier than the sword.

Turn right out of the car park and go up past the church and the Old Vicarage following the Oxfordshire Way. Where the track goes right to Chapel Wells (house), keep ahead through a gate (Walk 25 follows the bridleway between these two routes) and follow the left-hand fence down through two fields. Cross the track and follow the bridleway steeply up through Pishillbury Wood. A path joins from the left and after 75m the route then splits; fork left, following the Oxfordshire Way, down to a road at **Maidensgrove**.

Cross over and follow the signed bridleway uphill, keeping close to the right-hand side of the wood. Ignore a path to the right and keep ahead across the field, bear left along the right-hand hedge to a path junction just before Lodge Farm.

Follow the **Chiltern Way** leftwards across the field, keeping left of the wooden electricity pole, and then go down through Park Wood to a gate. Continue down through two fields (view ahead of Stonor House); at the far side of the second field go through a gate and along the enclosed path between houses to a road. Cross over

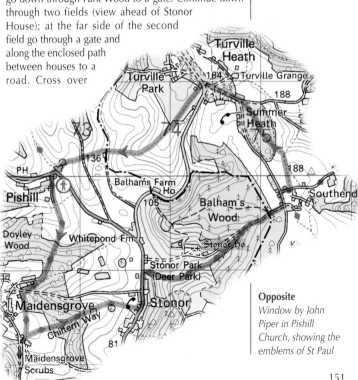

Opposite

Window by John Piper in Pishill Church, showing the emblems of St Paul

151

Park Wood in autumn colours

and turn left for 300m, passing a junction, to reach the deer fence on the right.

Turn right through the gate to enter **Stonor Park** and follow the path (Chiltern Way and Shakespeare's Way) up through the deer park for 1.1km past some trees, soon with views of **Stonor House** to the left.

> **Stonor House** has been the home of Lord and Lady Camoys and the Stonor family for over 800 years. The house, hidden in a fold of the Chilterns and surrounded by a deer park, started life in the late 1100s. By 1540 it had taken on a classic 'E' shape, with a Georgian brick façade later built over the original timber and flint structure. The Stonor family refused to renounce Catholicism and as a result Stonor became a refuge for Catholics, among them the Jesuit scholar and missionary Edmund Campion, executed in 1581 and later canonised. During this time the Stonor family were imprisoned

and deprived of their land, but they were later reinstated and their descendants still live here. For opening times call 01491 638587.

Keep to the path (white arrows on trees) and go through a gate to leave the deer park. Continue straight on up through Kildridge Wood, keeping ahead over the brow of the hill, and soon pass a gate and then some brick and flint cottages.

Turn left along the lane for 150m, and at the houses in Southend go right along the concrete track with a grassy area to the right and houses on the left for 125m. Just before the track junction turn left over a stile, keep ahead through two gates either side of a drive and continue along the left-hand field edge. In the distance to the right (north-east) you can see Cobstone Windmill (Walk 23) above Turville. Keep ahead through two gates to enter a large field, where the path splits.

Fork left to the trees, go through a gate and continue for 25m to reach a marker post and path junction; keep

The view east across the upper Hambleden Valley from near Summerheath Wood

The picturesque little church at Pishill is the starting point for Walks 24 and 25

At the second junction a bridleway on the right heads north to The Barn Café (250m each way).

ahead (north-west) through the trees of **Summer Heath**. After 300m pass through a fence gap and keep ahead at the crossing path (marker post), soon aiming for a house at **Turville Heath**. Turn left along the lane, keeping straight on at two road junctions. ◄

At the third junction (a skewed T-junction) go straight over to follow the driveway (footpath sign) to a house (Saviours), which soon curves left (south-west). Go through the gate and keep ahead (house over to the right) to reach a gate. Continue across the next field, passing just right of a tree; go through a gate in the hedge and continue through the field to another gate.

Turn right along the enclosed track and start descending, passing a seat by some trees with a great view. Continue steeply downhill, going straight over a crossing track (barn on left), and follow a line of trees to head up to a gate and another crossing track (Hollandridge Lane – Walk 25). Go straight over, following the enclosed path downhill for 350m, go through a gate and turn left along the track to the road beside Pishill Farmhouse. Turn right (west) for 50m and then go left across the road to follow the lane back to the church in **Pishill**. (The Crown Inn is 200m west along the main road.)

WALK 25

Pishill, Cookley Green and Russell's Water

Start/finish	Car park beside Pishill Church (SU 726 898), off the B480 just north of Stonor
Distance	14.3km (9 miles) or 10km (6¼ miles)
Ascent	410m or 335m
Time	4¼hrs or 3hrs
Maps	OS Explorer 171
Refreshments	Five Horsehoes (01491 641282) at Upper Maidensgrove; Crown Inn (01491 638364) at Pishill (detour)
Public transport	None

A fairly long walk, starting from Pishill and meandering through lovely beech woods and open common land. Along the way the walk passes the perfectly situated Five Horsehoes to reach Park Corner and Cookley Green. From here it heads to Russell's Water, with its picturesque pond, following the Chiltern Way to Hollandridge Farm before descending back to Pishill. A shorter route, missing out Park Corner, is also described.

From the church car park in Pishill turn right past The Old Vicarage, and where the drive curves right towards a house (Chapel Wells) and the Oxfordshire Way forks left (straight on) through a gate (route of Walk 24), take the bridleway half-right between the two. Head west and gently uphill, soon with Long Wood on the right, to reach a crossing path.

Turn left through a gate down alongside the field boundary; go through another gate and continue down through **Doyley Wood** to a dip and up the other side. Leave the trees and keep ahead between fences, and then between buildings, to follow a track to a minor road. Turn right for 1km (**Shakespeare's Way**) or, for a better option, head westwards across Russell's Water Common, aiming for the first house on the right-hand side of the road (SU 712 889).

Upper Maidensgrove, with its sister hamlet Maidensgrove, was known as Menygrove ('common clearing') in late medieval times. The village has the only pub on the route, with a great view from its garden.

Continue along the lane for a further 200m, passing the Five Horseshoes at **Upper Maidensgrove**, and immediately after a house (Periwinkle) on the left, turn left and follow the enclosed path (singposted Park Corner 1¼) downhill. Go through a gate and turn right to follow the right-hand field edge steeply down to a gate and a crossing bridleway.

Shortcut

Turn right and continue for 800m to reach a junction (SU 705 895). Turn right uphill, rejoining the main walk.

Turn left for 10m and then right through a gate (Chiltern Way) into the beech trees and follow the fence on the right through another gate. Continue alongside the fence for 150m,

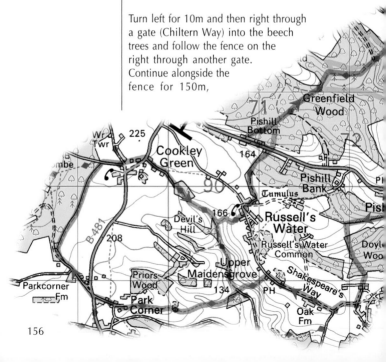

and as the fence falls away to the right bear slightly left, heading gently uphill. At the top, keep ahead into the next field and follow the right-hand field edge; go through a gate and continue straight on across the next field, soon following a fence on the right. Continue straight on through another gate, and after 150m cross a stile at the corner and join a tree-shaded bridleway. Turn left.

Heading north alongside Haycroft Wood

Soon join a lane just after passing Chears Farm, and continue straight on past the houses of **Park Corner** to a T-junction with the B481. Turn right for a few metres and with care turn left across the road and follow the lane for Ewelme Park and Swyncombe House. Keep ahead past **Parkcorner Farm** to reach a cottage, where the track splits; take the right-hand fork (bridleway to Cookley Green) passing to the right of the cottage.

Head north-north-east, with Haycroft Wood on the left, for 1km and then turn right along Church Lane (Chiltern Way) to a junction in **Cookley Green**.

At Cookley Green the houses nestle around a large triangular green where a number of lanes converge. The **village** was originally developed to house farm workers and servants from nearby Swyncombe (Walk 26), where a manor house, church, rectory and farm are located.

Go straight on across the common with houses to your left. Cross the B481, turn left for a few metres, then turn right down the track (Chiltern Way and Shakespeare Way); after the last house keep ahead down the bridleway for 750m to reach a junction (SU 705 895) and turn left. (The shorter walk rejoins here and both routes now follow the Chiltern Way to Hollandridge Farm.)

Follow the Chiltern Way uphill, later bearing left along the track to **Russell's Water** and turn left along the lane to the picturesque pond – which played a part in the film *Chitty Chitty Bang Bang*. Turn right along the track for 50m (pond on right) and go left along another track (Chiltern Way) with houses on the left. Keep ahead alongside the hedge, with trees to your right, to reach Russell's Water Common. Turn left, following the edge of the grassy common to the corner, and descend through oak and beech trees, keeping close to the left edge at first. Later continue down the drive to the road at **Pishill Bottom** where there is a choice of two routes.

Permissive route

Cross over and follow the permissive bridleway up through Shambridge Wood for 250m to a junction (SU 710 905). Turn right (Chiltern Way).

For the official right of way, cross over, turn left along the road for 300m to Grove Farm and turn right through the gate. Follow the track between barns, and after curving right, fork left up beside the fence and up through the trees. (The permissive route soon joins from the right.)

Continue north-eastwards, soon following a track; keep ahead at the junction to follow the track (Chiltern Way) down to a dip in **Greenfield Wood** and then up the

other side to a crossing track. Go straight on, downhill, and cross two tracks at the bottom of the slope before following the Chiltern Way up through College Wood. After 150m the route bears right and starts heading gently down to a dip and track junction. Cross diagonally left and follow the path up to a junction near the top of the wood and go left; cross a stile and continue through the field to a track.

Hollandridge Farm – from here the route follows Hollandridge Lane back down to Pishill

Turn right past **Hollandridge Farm** and follow Hollandridge Lane (surfaced track) for 1.4km down to a crossing path (Walk 24). Turn right, following the path downhill, then go through a gate and turn left along the track to the road beside Pishill Farmhouse. Turn right for 50m (200m further along the road from here is The Crown Inn) then go left across the road to follow the lane back up to the church in **Pishill**. If you have the time you might like to take a look inside the church, which features some interesting stained glass windows (see Walk 24).

WALK 26
Ewelme and Swyncombe

Start/finish	Car park at the recreation ground in Ewelme beside Cow Common (SU 648 911)
Distance	11.6km (7¼ miles)
Ascent	310m
Time	3½hrs
Map	OS Explorer 171
Refreshments	Shepherds Hut Pub (01491 836636) and shop with tearoom (01491 834467) at Ewelme (short detour)
Public transport	Bus services to RAF Benson (Green Lane, SU 638 917 – near the Shepherds Hut Pub) from Cholsey and Wallingford

The walk, which starts from the peaceful and historic Oxfordshire village of Ewelme, nestling below the Chiltern Hills, heads for Ewelme Park before arriving at Swyncombe – home to the very attractive St Botolph's Church. The return route includes sweeping views along the Chiltern scarp from Swyncombe Downs before descending back to Ewelme.

From the back of the car park go through two gates and head south-east across **Cow Common**, keeping close to the left-hand hedge at first and later going half-right across the field to a gate. Cross the lane and follow the tree-shaded bridleway (Grindon Lane) for 900m, later gently rising to a T-junction.

Turn left and go down to a cross-junction with the Swan's Way. Keep ahead, following a hedge line on the left through **Ewelme Downs**, and soon continue up alongside the fence before passing into another field and following the right-hand hedge up to its top right corner. Keep ahead along the track for 200m to reach a cross-junction at **Ewelme Park** – at one time a Royal hunting ground.

Turn left along the Ridgeway, and after passing a large barn follow the track to the right for 250m, continue along the right-hand field boundary heading north-east. At the field corner fork right, cross the stile into Swyncombe Park and follow the right-hand fence for 800m. Cross the stile at the corner to enter Haycroft Wood and bear half-left, soon crossing a surfaced drive. Keep ahead through the trees, soon with a fence on the left and grassy ride to the right, to a junction and fork left down through the trees to another junction (Chiltern Way). Turn left, go through a gate and head west across the parkland towards **Swyncombe House**. Continue through a gate by some trees, keep ahead across the drive and soon turn right through a gate into the churchyard. Go past the church and leave through a gate.

Stained glass window detail in St Botolph's Church, Swyncombe

The name **Swyncombe** is derived from the Old English *swin*, meaning 'wild boar', and *cumb*, or 'valley'. After 1066, William the Conqueror delegated responsibility for his new kingdom to trusted officers and friends, and, according to the Domesday Book, Milo Crispin was entrusted with Wallingford Castle, which included the estate of Swyncombe. Following the wars with France, **Swyncombe House** – which had connections with the Abbey of Bec in Normandy – passed through various owners, including Thomas Chaucer and his wife. The lovely little St Botolph's Church is of early Norman origin, with a distinctive semi-circular apse at the end of the nave and a plain Anglo-Saxon font.

Turn right along the track to a junction and go left up past The Old Rectory, following both the Ridgeway and Chiltern Way. Cross over Church Lane, go through a gate and down to a dip, then continue uphill and over the brow of the hill to arrive at a marker post (SU 682 914) just after passing an old earthwork. Turn left, following the Chiltern Way (earthwork on left).

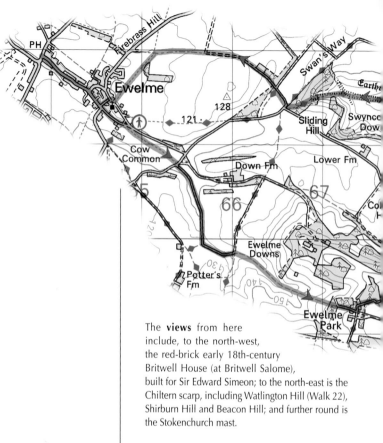

The **views** from here
include, to the north-west,
the red-brick early 18th-century
Britwell House (at Britwell Salome),
built for Sir Edward Simeon; to the north-east is the
Chiltern scarp, including Watlington Hill (Walk 22),
Shirburn Hill and Beacon Hill; and further round is
the Stokenchurch mast.

At a path junction fork left, go through a gate and
continue along the earthwork to another gate. Head
steeply down through the trees to arrive at a cross-track
junction beside a parking area and minor road. With the
road to your left, and **Swan's Way** off to the right along
the edge of Ickneild Bank Plantation, head north-west
along the track between open fields (Chiltern Way). Keep
ahead at the junction, soon passing a house, and after the
brow of the hill, where the track turns right, go straight on
between hedges for 600m to a crossing path. Turn half-left
through the gap and head diagonally south-west across

the field. Go through the fence gap beside the trees and keep ahead, following the enclosed path for 200m, later heading down to a driveway and minor road with St Mary's Church opposite. Turn right and then left down Burrows Hill (footpath) to The Street in **Ewelme**.

For the village store and tea-room – situated beside King's Pool, where the Ewelme Brook rises (and reputedly where Henry VIII bathed) – or the old watercress beds (now cared for by the Chiltern Society) or the Shepherds Hut pub, turn right along the road for 200m, 500m or 800m respectively; there is a bus stop 200m south-west from the pub. To return to the car park, turn left and keep left (straight on) at the junction for 300m, passing the almshouses and school.

Take a short detour to see the old watercress beds – now a local nature reserve

EWELME

Detail of Alice Chaucer's tomb

Picturesque Ewelme has a church, almshouses and school that were all founded in the 1430s by the Duke and Duchess of Suffolk. The school is believed to be the oldest in the country in continuous use. St Mary's Church has a stunningly detailed effigy of Alice Chaucer (d.1475) – who became the Duchess of Suffolk following her marriage to William de la Pole (d.1450), 1st Duke of Suffolk – as well as the altar tomb of Thomas Chaucer (d.1434), son of the famous poet Geoffrey Chaucer, and his wife Matilda Burghersh (d.1436) who had inherited the manor of Ewelme from her father. The manor, later known as 'Ewelme Palace', passed to the Crown and was visited on several occasions by Henry VIII (who built a hunting lodge at Ewelme Park) and Elizabeth I. Only part of the 'palace' remains on the site of the present Georgian manor house.

The churchyard is the resting place of *Three Men in a Boat* author Jerome K Jerome (1859–1927), and the village was where Tony Rowse started keeping bees in 1938, later forming the well-known Rowse Honey Company, which moved to Wallingford in 1954.

WALK 27

Checkendon and Stoke Row

Start/finish	Checkendon church (SU 663 830); limited roadside parking
Distance	12km (7½ miles)
Ascent	300m
Time	3½hrs
Maps	OS Explorer 171
Refreshments	Crooked Billet (01491 681048), Cherry Tree Inn (01491 680430) and village shop at Stoke Row
Public transport	None

From the lovely village of Checkendon the route heads through woods and open countryside, with a view from Berrins Hill across the Oxfordshire plain. After passing English Farm it then goes through Stoke Row, taking in the rather unusual Maharajah's Well before heading back to Checkendon.

Church of St Peter and St Paul, Checkendon

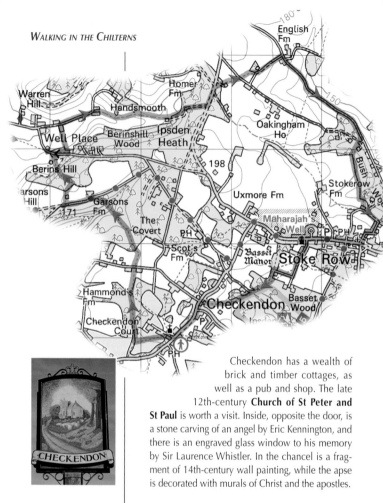

Checkendon has a wealth of brick and timber cottages, as well as a pub and shop. The late 12th-century **Church of St Peter and St Paul** is worth a visit. Inside, opposite the door, is a stone carving of an angel by Eric Kennington, and there is an engraved glass window to his memory by Sir Laurence Whistler. In the chancel is a fragment of 14th-century wall painting, while the apse is decorated with murals of Christ and the apostles.

Stand facing Checkendon church and follow the gravel drive towards **Checkendon Court**, passing to the left of the church. Just before the wrought iron gates turn left through a gate; follow the right-hand fence and then keep ahead across the field. Go through two gates and turn right along the enclosed path with a field on your left. Keep ahead through the trees for 300m to reach a

T-junction and turn left, soon bearing right (north) and staying just inside the trees.

Keep ahead to a minor road by some houses, cross over and go through a gate to continue across the field to a gate. Just inside the wood bear right and then left and follow the path through the trees (white arrows), heading north-west for 250m. Bear left down a stony track to a track junction in the dip and take the narrow lane opposite, heading up through the trees to join a minor road opposite **Garsons Farm**.

Turn left for 300m and then go right on a track (Chiltern Way) towards the house and farm shop. At the gate, fork slightly left along the parallel path, and once in the trees bear half-right to a three-way junction (SU 652 846). Go left for a few metres and then fork left (north-west) on a path, heading down **Berins Hill** (white arrows) to a gate with a view out over Oxfordshire.

Continue downhill (Chiltern Way), go through a gate and follow the right-hand field edge down to a track. Cross the minor road and bear right, going up through the trees and keeping parallel with the road for 100m. Turn left, go through a gate and head down towards **Well Place**; keep ahead across the gravel area and turn right along the lane (later a track) up the valley for 1.7km, passing Lower Handsmooth Farm and Handsmooth House up to the left. Later keep ahead along the track to pass **Ispden Heath** (owned by the Woodland Trust).

Cross the road and turn left for 200m, and once level with the access road to **Homer Farm** (left) fork half-right on a path through the trees, crossing a track to reach a stile. Follow the right-hand field edge to a corner and then continue, aiming slightly right across the field. Cross stiles either side of the surfaced drive that leads to **Oakingham House** and head across the field, aiming for the house and trees. Turn right over a stile and follow the left-hand hedge. Go left along the drive, passing a pond, and as the drive curves left towards the house, fork right into a field (cattle grid). Follow the left-hand field boundary and continue down to a track at **English Farm**.

Turn right for 25m and then fork right along the hedge-lined track (English Lane, signposted to Witheridge Hill), heading downhill for 1.2km to reach a surfaced track at a bend. Turn right for 25m, and at the entrance to a house on the left (Donnelly), where the track curves right and rises, fork left (straight on) along a path up through the trees with a fence on the left (signposted 'Stoke Row 1').

At the top, bear left through a gate and follow the enclosed path close to the edge of **Bush Wood** for 400m. Keep ahead down to a dip and then up again, with houses and fence to your left. Go through a gate and continue straight on (southwards) to pass between buildings

Maharajah's Well,
Stoke Row

at the 17th-century Crooked Billet pub. Turn left along the lane, which soon curves right up to the main road in **Stoke Row**, beside the village common.

Turn right, passing The Cherry Tree Inn, village shop, cherry orchard and the **Maharajah's Well**.

Stoke Row is home to a rather unusual sight. Local man Edward Anderdon Reade, Governor of the North-West Provinces, had worked with the Maharajah of Benares in India during the early 19th century. Part of his work included sinking a **well** for a local community, and in 1863 the Maharajah decided to repay Reade's generosity by commissioning a well to be dug at Stoke Row. The well, which is 112m deep, displays its Indian heritage with its ornate cupola and gilded elephant. Close to the well is a cherry orchard that was also provided by the Maharajah.

Just before the church, turn left across the road and follow School Lane for 200m to a cross-track junction at the end of the houses. Just ahead a path forks half-right through the field; however, a better option is to follow the track straight on for 100m and turn right on a permissive path between fences. At the end go left and follow the fence on the left past some buildings. Continue through **Ipsden Wood**, soon following the fence on the right as it curves gently right down to a house in the dip at the junction with Judges Road.

Go straight on, following the right-hand fence uphill. Go through a gate and keep ahead through two fields to reach a gate tucked in the far right corner of the second field. Follow the enclosed path past gardens, turn left and follow the road, passing two junctions, back to the church in **Checkendon**.

WALK 28
Hailey and Grim's Ditch

Start/finish	Junction of Ridgeway and minor road, 1km south of the A4130 east of Crowmarsh Gifford (SU 635 875); limited parking
Distance	9.5km (6 miles)
Ascent	210m
Time	2¾hrs
Map	OS Explorer 171
Refreshments	The King William (01491 681845) at Hailey
Public transport	Bus links to Nuffield (SU 675 877) from Henley-on-Thames and Oxford (1.3km detour each way following the Ridgeway)

The first part of the walk follows the Chiltern Way to the little hamlet of Hailey. From here it follows a good track up past Bixmoor Wood before heading northwards to meet the Ridgeway – at which point a detour may be made to visit the 12th-century Holy Trinity Church in Nuffield. The final section follows the Ridgeway alongside the ancient earthwork of Grim's Ditch back to the start.

Look out for this sign near the start of the walk

Follow the minor road southwards for 350m and then turn left towards **Woodhouse Farm** for 450m, following the Chiltern Way. On drawing level with the farmhouse, turn right and go up through the trees of **Wicks Wood**. Where the track curves left, keep ahead along the path and shortly leave the trees; continue straight on across the field and along the track, soon passing some farm buildings at **Poors Farm**. Continue south along the track to **Hailey**, and at the T-junction, beside Stone Farm, turn left to The King William pub.

Follow the track uphill to pass through **Bixmoor Wood**, keeping left at a junction (SU 653 860), and continue along the main track, later passing a couple of houses as you head towards **Homer Farm**.

After passing a large barn (left) and The Old
Farmhouse (right), turn left past a gate (signposted
'Nuffield 1½'). Keep to the right of a large wooden barn
(workshop) and follow the path across a gravel drive with
a house to the right. Continue past the trees, pass a gate
and follow the left-hand fence. Go through a gate and
keep ahead across the field; cross the drive and keep
ahead towards **Ridgeway Farmhouse**. Turn right alongside the hedge and fence to reach a stile; cross the drive
and follow the enclosed path, which quickly turns left.
On leaving the bushes, beside a wooden electricity pole,
go slightly left into the left-hand field and follow the
hedge on the right. Continue down through the trees to a
junction with the Ridgeway.

Detour to Holy Trinity Church

To visit the church in Nuffield (which features a Norman
font with carved inscription and a 14th-century floor
brass in memory of Benet English), go straight on uphill,
continue along the right-hand field margin to a gate and
turn right along the lane for 100m (church on right).
Retrace your steps to return to the main route and then
turn right. (For public transport, continue along the
Ridgeway to the A4130.)

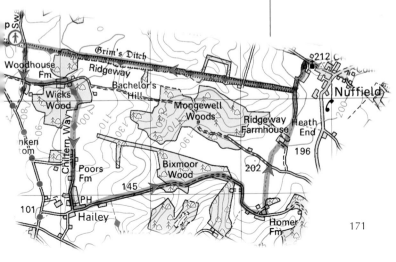

171

The final part of the walk follows Grim's Ditch, passing through Oaken Copse

During late spring and early summer the wood – like many Chiltern woods – is carpeted with bluebells.

Turn left and follow the Ridgeway down alongside the tree-shaded **Grim's Ditch** for 3km back to the start, crossing a track with a house to the left and later passing through Oaken Copse. ◄

> **Grim's Ditch** is a well-defined west-east linear ridge stretching from the River Thames to Nuffield (although the name is shared with a number of prehistoric earthworks). The earthwork probably dates from the Iron Age, and was most likely built to mark a boundary rather than as a defensive structure. The word 'Grim' is one of the Anglo-Saxon names for Woden (known as Odin by the Norse) – 'the masked one'.

WALK 29
Nettlebed and Nuffield

Start/finish	Nettlebed village green, near the junction of the A4130 and B481 (SU 701 867); roadside parking
Distance	14.6km (9 miles) or 12.8km (8 miles)
Ascent	310m or 235m
Time	4hrs or 3½hrs
Maps	OS Explorer 171
Refreshments	White Hart (01491 641245), The Field Kitchen deli-café (01491 641831) and shop in Nettlebed
Public transport	Daily bus services to Nettlebed from Henley-on-Thames and Oxford

An undulating walk exploring the varied countryside around Nettlebed, at one time known for its brick-making industry. Along the way the route passes Nuffield Place, former home of Lord Nuffield, before exploring Warburg Nature Reserve on the way back to Nettlebed. A slightly shorter version, also described, misses out the nature reserve.

Before leaving the green in Nettlebed, take a look at the puddingstones (a type of conglomerate rock) and the old kiln. Then head west along the High Street (A4130), crossing over Watlington Street (B481) and passing The White Hart. Cross at the traffic lights and continue past The Field Kitchen café.

> **Nettlebed** was once noted for its brick-making, which was done using local deposits of clay; one of the old 18th-century bottle kilns, overlooking the village green, has been preserved. Most of St Bartholomew's Church in the village dates from the 1840s, although parts of the tower are Norman. There are several memorials to members of the Fleming family – who at one time lived at Joyce

The old brick kiln at Nettlebed

Grove – including a colourful stained glass window by John Piper in memory of Peter Fleming (1907–1971) – writer, traveller, soldier and elder brother of the *James Bond* author Ian Fleming.

Just past St Bartholomew's Church, turn left along a narrow path between the fence and brick wall, then keep ahead along the track past the farm buildings for 800m (the track soon becomes surfaced). At the right-hand bend go straight on into the trees for a few metres and then turn right down the bridleway.

Rejoin the surfaced track at the bottom of the hill and turn left, later following it as it bends right towards **Howberrywood**. At the buildings fork right, keeping the buildings to the left, and follow the track as it curves right then left, with trees to your left. Where the track bends right towards **Hayden Farm** go straight on along the tree-shaded bridleway, heading north-west for 1.2km to **Nuffield**.

As the track swings right beside a cottage, take the narrow path ahead beside the left-hand hedge; cross diagonally left over the road and continue along Nuffield Hill. Just before the **church**, turn sharp right along the Ridgeway, passing through two fields.

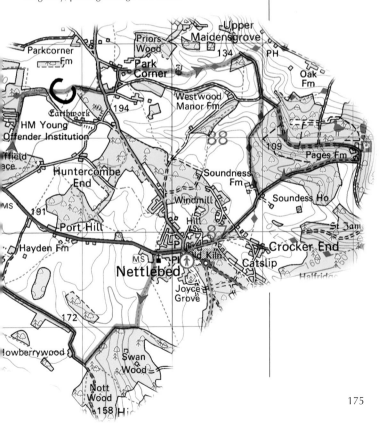

Holy Trinity Church in Nuffield dates from the 12th century, with the tower and north aisle added around the 14th century. Inside there is a Norman font with carved inscription and a 14th-century floor brass in memory of Benet English. William Richard Morris, aka Lord Nuffield (1877–1963), benefactor of Nuffield College, Oxford and founder of Morris Motors, is buried in the churchyard.

Keep left of the clubhouse and follow the white-topped posts across the golf course (watch out for flying golf balls). After passing through some trees, keep ahead across two fairways separated by a belt of trees and follow the path past a house. Bear right along the gravel drive to arrive at the main road.

Carefully cross the A4130 and turn right past the bus stop, then left along the lane (Bradley Road), continuing for 300m to reach a footpath sign. Go right, following the gravel drive between buildings, and keep ahead between hedges; soon a crossing path and gate on the right gives access to **Nuffield Place** (when open).

Holy Trinity Church, Nuffield

NUFFIELD PLACE

This attractive country residence was the home of philanthropist **William Richard Morris**, Lord Nuffield, from 1933 until his death in 1963. Morris, said to be one of the most remarkable men of the 20th century, started his business career repairing bicycles before branching out into motorcycle manufacture and repair and designing the Morris Motor Cycle. This was quickly followed by the first Morris Garage (the initials of which were used for the MG sports car brand) and within a few years he started producing cars, the first being the two-seater Morris Oxford 'Bullnose' in 1913. By 1925 the company was producing 56,000 cars per year. Morris Motors Ltd later became part of BMC and then British Leyland. For more information about National Trust-owned Nuffield Place, including opening times, call 01491 641224.

Continue straight on to a junction beside Park Wood. Go left, following the left-hand field edge and soon passing alongside the **HM Young Offender Institution** (left). After the houses on the left, dogleg left into the trees and continue northwards to a cross junction. Turn right (east) along the Chiltern Way. After 300m, keep left (straight on) at the split and continue, soon passing a wood, to a road (B481). With care, cross over and turn right then left along the road for **Park Corner**. Follow the lane as it bends left and continue for 250m to the next left bend.

Turn right along the track (Chiltern Way and Russell's Water 1¼) for 175m and turn right over a stile. Follow the path along the left-hand edge through three fields. Enter the fourth field and follow the Chiltern Way downhill, staying right of some trees and later following the left-hand boundary (this section is used by Walk 25). Go through a gate and continue through the trees to pass another gate. Turn right along the track for 500m to a track junction (SU 709 884).

Shortcut

Keep ahead through a gate, following the Chiltern Way south up across the field; go through another gate and continue up beside the trees. In the next field turn left, following the field edge and a track to a surfaced drive. Turn right to rejoin the main route.

Turn left and shortly enter Warburg Nature Reserve. Follow the track along the wooded valley for 1.2km to the visitor centre (right); on the way a waymarked nature trail on the left explores the nature reserve and rejoins the walk near the visitor centre.

> The BBOWT **Warburg Nature Reserve**, offering a mix of flower-rich grassland and ancient woodland, is named after the late Oxford University botanist Dr E F Warburg (1908–1966). Facilities include a visitor centre, toilets, bird hide and a waymarked wildlife walk (01491 642001).

Keep to the surfaced track as it curves right (south) and turn right after **Pages Farm**, following the track uphill. After 600m fork left at the junction, heading more steeply uphill, and join a lane near **Soundess House** (where the shortcut rejoins). Keep ahead and later fork right to return to **Nettlebed**.

WALK 30

Greys Green, Rotherfield Greys and Greys Court

Start/finish	Greys Green Village Hall, west of Henley-on-Thames (SU 720 829); limited parking
Distance	7.2km (4½ miles)
Ascent	130m
Time	2hrs
Map	OS Explorer 171
Refreshments	Maltsters Arms (01491 628400) at Rotherfield Greys; tearoom at Greys Court (National Trust, 01491 628529)
Public transport	Limited bus service (excluding weekends) to Greys Green and Rotherfield Greys from Henley-on-Thames

A short walk that meanders through beech woods and open countryside just to the north-west of Henley-on-Thames, passing through the neighbouring villages of Greys Green and Rotherfield Greys. Pop inside the Church of St Nicholas in Rotherfield Greys to see an ancient brass and a magnificent monument, and allow time to visit historic Greys Court.

From Greys Green village hall turn left alongside the road with the cricket pitch and village green on your right. Continue past a road junction, and after the last house on the left turn left through a gate, heading south-east along the enclosed **Chiltern Way** with a golf course on your right for 900m, ignoring a crossing track. Follow the route as it swings right, continue for 125m and go left through a gate. Head across the fields, passing through three gates, and follow the enclosed path alongside the churchyard wall to the road in **Rotherfield Greys**. (To the left is the Maltsters Arms.)

The **Church of St Nicholas** in Rotherfield Greys, which probably stands on the site of the original Saxon church, dates back to Norman times – albeit having undergone a lot of Victorian restoration.

179

Inside there are several memorials to past owners of Greys Court, including a fine brass of Robert de Grey (d.1387), a founder Knight of the Garter. The Knollys Chapel was added in 1605 and houses a magnificent monument to Sir Francis Knollys (1514–1596) and his wife Katherine (although she is buried at Westminster Abbey); around the base are smaller effigies of 14 of their children, while on top are the kneeling effigies of their second son William (later Earl of Banbury) and his wife. William is believed to have been the role model for Shakespeare's Malvolio in *Twelfth Night*.

Turn right past the lych gate and then go left across the road and through a gate into the field, where the path splits. Take the left fork straight across to a stile and descend through the Pindars Wood – a great place for bluebells – to cross a stile. Turn right, following the field edge through two fields. In the third field turn left and follow the left-hand field margin up to the top left corner, then bear right along the enclosed track. Keep ahead along the concrete track to reach a road; turn right along the verge and continue for 75m before going left across the road and over a stile. Follow the left-hand field edge and go straight on across the field, then keep ahead with the hedge on your left and soon follow a line of trees. Cross a stile to enter **Lambridge Wood**.

Keep ahead for 50m to a path junction (marker post) and turn left (heading northwest with an old earth-work on

the left). Keep ahead at the next waymarked junction for 150m to another marker post at a cross junction. (There are a number of minor paths in the wood, potentially making route-finding difficult.) Turn left and follow the path for 850m through the beech wood, firstly going west and then south-west (passing close to the edge of the wood for a while) to reach a minor road with the houses of **Broadplat** to the left. Cross over and go through the trees to a track junction. Turn left beside a wooden electricity pole, following the path beside the fence with the buildings on your right.

Go left through a gate and then quickly right through another and continue alongside the fence on the left (soon the Chiltern Way joins from the right and the route follows this back to Greys Green). Keep ahead over a footbridge and soon pass through a gate before continuing alongside the fence on the right. Keep ahead through the car park to a surfaced drive, then turn right past the kiosk and entrance to **Greys Court**.

Heading towards Lambridge Wood

GREYS COURT

The estate dates back to the time of the Domesday Book, when it was owned by the de Grey family; it was during their time that the manor house was fortified. Part of the curtain wall and tower survive, the latter giving a good view of the garden. The manor was granted by Henry VII to Robert Knollys in 1514, and the family re-used much of the original stone to build the present Tudor house. The estate later passed to Sir William Stapleton through marriage; his son Sir Thomas was a cousin of Sir Francis Dashwood of Hellfire Club fame (Walk 20). The final owners were Sir Felix and Lady Brunner, who gave the estate to the National Trust. As well as the interesting house, the walled garden has a magnificent wisteria; there is also a Tudor donkey-wheel-operated well, a 19th-century icehouse and a modern brick maze.

Keep to the surfaced drive, ignoring two drives to the right, and as it curves left go straight on through a gate to a minor road. Cross straight over, go through a gate and follow the Chiltern Way south-westwards across the field. Start rising and keep ahead through a gate; continue up through the trees, passing through another gate. Keep ahead to reach the cricket pitch in **Greys Green** and bear left along the track to go back to the village hall.

6 ALONG THE THAMES

A peaceful scene on the River Thames at Medmenham (Walk 31)

WALK 31

Hambleden, Medmenham and the River Thames

Start/finish	Car park 400m north of Mill End and the A4155 (SU 785 854) via Skirmett Road
Distance	13.6km (8½ miles)
Ascent	270m
Time	3¾hrs
Map	OS Explorer 171
Refreshments	Stag and Huntsman (01491 571227) and village shop with tearoom at Hambleden; Dog and Badger (01491 579944) at Medmenham
Public transport	Regular bus links to Mill End and Medmenham from High Wycombe and Henley-on-Thames/Reading

The walk passes through the scenic Hambleden valley to the north of Henley-on-Thames, visiting the pretty village of Hambleden. Then it heads through open fields and lovely beech woods, passing a former Iron Age fort, to reach Medmenham. The final section follows the peaceful River Thames towards Mill End and back to the car park.

The stream is known as a winterbourne – it usually only flows following heavy, sustained winter rainfall.

From the car park turn right (south) towards Mill End and continue for 50m to reach the junction for Rotten Row. Turn sharp left, doubling back through a gate, and follow the path north through the field, parallel to the road. Keep ahead through gates either side of a farm track, heading for **Hambleden**. Turn right along the road – crossing the bridge over the Hamble Brook – to reach the village centre, with the shop/tearoom and St Mary's Church to the left. ◄

Keep right (straight on) at the junction and continue past the Stag and Huntsman and car park to a junction and turn right for 150m. At the end of the wall turn left, following the Chiltern Way and Shakespeare's Way up the left-hand field edge. Keep ahead through the trees, and a few metres after crossing a track go through a gate.

HAMBLEDEN

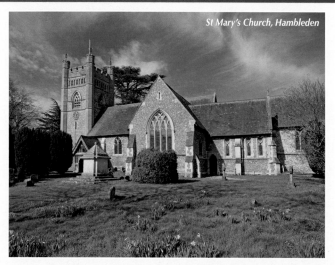

St Mary's Church, Hambleden

Picturesque Hambleden, with 400-year old cottages clustered round the church, has seen its fair share of film action over the years, including *Chitty Chitty Bang Bang* (1968) and *Sleepy Hollow* (1999) as well as TV appearances in *Midsomer Murders* and *New Tricks*. St Mary's Church dates back 800 years; inside there is the rather grand D'Oyley Memorial to Sir Cope D'Oyley (d.1633), his wife Martha (d.1618) and their 10 children. There is also a 16th-century oak altar, known as the Wolsey Altar, whose wood panelling bears the coat of arms of Cardinal Wolsey.

In the churchyard is the grave of Victorian bookseller and government minister W H Smith, the first Viscount Hambleden (1825–1891). The first William Henry Smith (1792–1865) lent his name to the family empire, which started out as a small newsagent shop on The Strand, London. Famous sons of the village include James Thomas Brudenell (1797–1868), 7th Earl of Cardigan (later Lord Cardigan), who led the famous Charge of the Light Brigade at Balaclava during the Crimean War (1854), and St Thomas de Cantilupe (1218–1282), Bishop of Hereford and the last Englishman to be canonised before the Reformation.

Follow the left-hand field edge, then keep ahead and slightly right across the field (east) to cross a track and continue between fields to a gate. Turn left along the lane to **Rotten Row** and, where the lane goes left, keep ahead between a barn (left) and houses (right).

On the left is Homefield Wood Nature Reserve – a good place for orchids and butterflies.

Continue through two fields, then through a gate and some trees; bear right along the lane for 150m. Turn sharp left, following Chiltern Way down through **Heath Wood**. Turn right along the valley for 1.1km to reach a road. ◀ Turn right for 20m and then turn left and follow the enclosed path downhill as it shortly swings right and

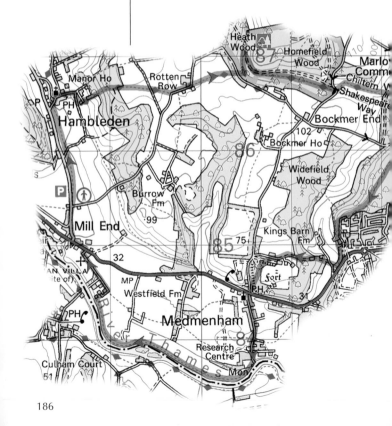

Following the Chiltern Way towards Pullingshill Wood

continues to enter Pullingshill Wood (Woodland Trust). Keep ahead up to a path junction just before a minor road. ▶

Turn right, following an old ditch line for 475m; cross a minor road, turn right downhill for 15m and take the lower of two waymarked paths heading south-west through Hollowhill and Hog Wood, keeping along the crest with the slope to your right (ignore all side routes). On reaching houses bear right, staying in the wood, and later (just after a flint wall) bear left to a drive. Turn right down the drive, and just before the houses on the right turn right through the hedge. Follow the fence downhill to a path junction and turn left. Later bear right. Leave the trees and turn right along the drive to a three-way split; take the left-hand drive up past a house. Keep ahead, following the bridleway alongside the wall and fence. Bear right along the track (later surfaced), pass The Old School, and once level with The Old Laundry (house) turn left.

Cross the drive and take the track opposite for 25m before turning right into the trees. ▶

An information board gives details about the extensive former WWI training trenches that can still be seen in the woods.

The route now passes through the northern earthworks of a fort known as Medmenham Camp – a former Iron Age hill fort built on a defensive site above the River Thames.

187

Continue south-south-west through the trees, passing through the western rampart, and follow the path steeply down to the crossroads in **Medmenham**. To your right is The Dog and Badger and straight across is the church.

> **Medmenham**, which stretches along Ferry Lane down to the river, is home to the Norman Church of St Peter and St Paul, built under the patronage of Hugh de Bolebec II in the 12th century. The ruins of the nearby former Cistercian Abbey of St Mary were used to build a house (private) that was once owned by Sir Francis Dashwood, who hosted meetings of the 'Monks of Medmenham' (forerunner to the infamous Hellfire Club – see Walk 20) here.

Cross straight over the road (A4155) and follow Ferry Lane to the **River Thames**.

Bear right over the footbridge, passing a **monument** commemorating the ferry that used to cross the river here,

Church of St Peter and St Paul in Medmenham

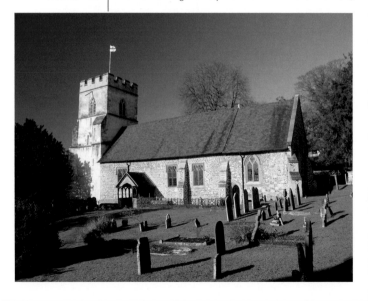

and continue alongside the river for 2.3km, later passing a small island, or eyot, in the river and then the imposing 18th-century **Culham Court** on the opposite bank. On reaching a house at the field corner turn right, away from the river, following the path along the field boundary for 150m. Turn left through a gate and follow the surfaced track to the A4155 at **Mill End**. With care, turn left for 100m (narrow verge) before crossing over and continuing along the pavement. Turn right at the junction and follow Skirmett Road for 400m back to the **car park**.

The River Thames near Medmenham

WALK 32

Henley-on-Thames and Middle Assendon

Start/finish	Bridge over the River Thames in Henley-on-Thames (SU 763 826; pay-and-display parking nearby), or Henley railway station (SU 763 822). Car drivers could also start at the car park near Mill End (SU 785 854)
Distance	18.5km (11½ miles)
Ascent	375m
Time	5½hrs
Map	OS Explorer 171
Refreshments	Plenty of choice at Henley-on-Thames; The Rainbow (01491 574879) at Middle Assendon
Public transport	Henley-on-Thames has trains to Twyford (mainline) and bus links to High Wycombe and Reading

From quaint Henley-on-Thames, famed for its regatta, the walk follows the River Thames past Temple Island before crossing the river at Hambleden Lock and rising up into the Chilterns. After admiring the views across the Stonor Valley, the return leg drops down through Middle Assendon and heads back to Henley-on-Thames following part of the Oxfordshire Way.

HENLEY-ON-THAMES

The prosperous and historic market town of Henley-on-Thames, described by Charles Dickens as 'the Mecca of the rowing man', has been linked with rowing since the first boat race between Cambridge and Oxford in 1829. Ten years later the regatta was formed, gaining Royal patronage in 1851, and is now held annually in early July. The town is home to The Leander Club, claimed to be the world's oldest rowing club, as well as the award-winning River and Rowing Museum (01491 415600) close to the railway station. St Mary's Parish Church, which dates from the early 1200s (although it was rebuilt on a grander scale during the 15th century), contains some good Victorian stained glass windows.

▶ Follow the A4130 east across the River Thames and shortly turn left along the enclosed path, passing the Leander Club. Follow the **Thames Path** for 3.7km downstream past **Remenham** to **Hambleden Lock**.

To reach the start point from the railway station, turn right and then right again along Station Road to the river, and follow the road northwards to the bridge (450m each way).

This beautiful stretch of the Thames offers several **points of interest**: just before Remenham look left across the river to see the elegant brick façade of the 17-century Fawley Court, reputedly designed by Sir Christopher Wren. Next is Temple Island with its elegant folly, designed by James Wyatt in 1771 and built as a summerhouse and fishing lodge for Fawley Court. The island also marks the start of the regatta course, where boats race upstream along the 2112-metre course known as the Henley Reach – the longest straight stretch on the river. Further on, again across the river, is the early 19th-century white Italianate Greenlands, once home to Viscount Hambleden (aka William Henry Smith – the name behind the famous chain of newsagents).

Hambleden Mill

map continues
on page195

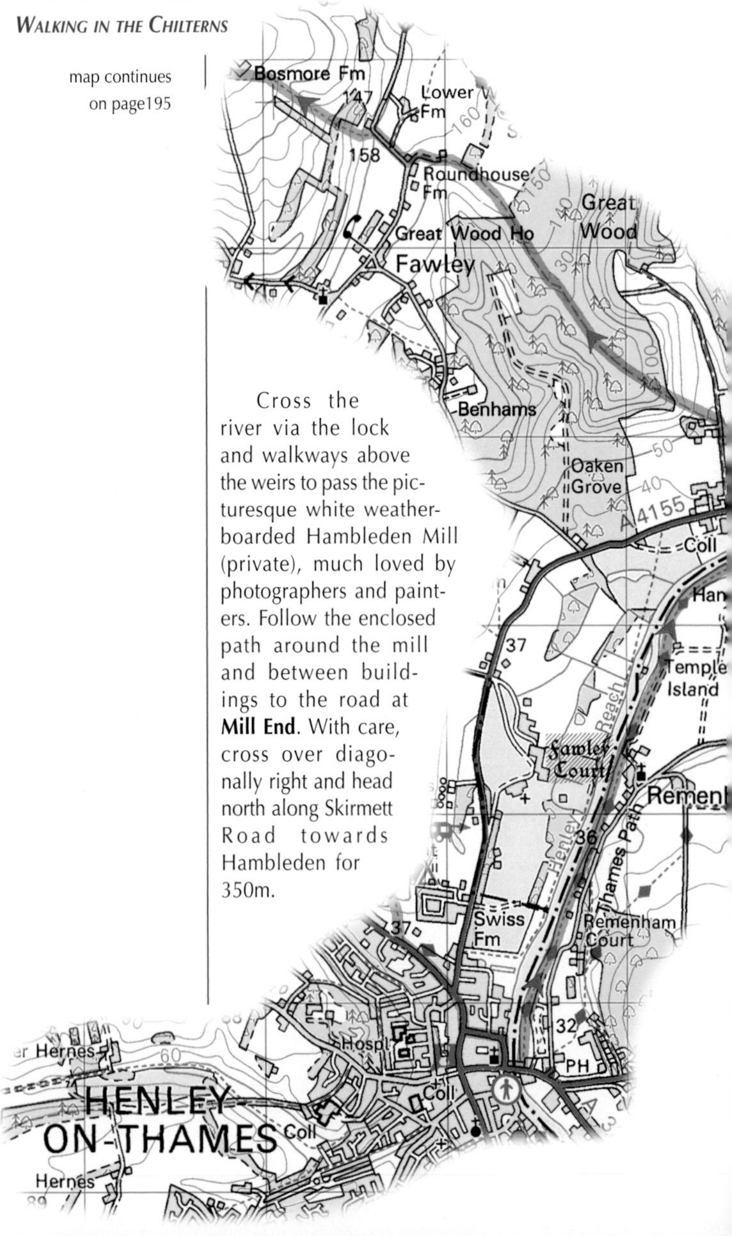

Cross the river via the lock and walkways above the weirs to pass the picturesque white weatherboarded Hambleden Mill (private), much loved by photographers and painters. Follow the enclosed path around the mill and between buildings to the road at **Mill End**. With care, cross over diagonally right and head north along Skirmett Road towards Hambleden for 350m.

The following labels appear on the map:

Bosmore Fm

Lower Fm

147

158

Roundhouse Fm

Great Wood Ho

Great Wood

Fawley

Benhams

Oaken Grove

A4155

Coll

Han

37

Temple Island

Fawley Court

Remen

36

Remenham Court

Swiss Fm

37

Hernes

Hospl

Coll

PH

32

HENLEY-
ON-THAMES

Coll

Hernes

At the junction for Rotten Row, leave the road and go through the gate ahead. Continue northwards through the field, keeping parallel to the road on your left. (Further along Skirmett Road is the car park that can be used as an alternative start – SU 785 854.) Go through a gate, turn left along the track to the road and turn right for 100m. Once past the third house, turn left across the road and follow the track (bridleway) up behind the houses. Continue just inside the southern edge of Ridge Wood, ignore a crossing route and later keep ahead past bushes, still following the bridleway, to reach a junction with a broad track.

Turn right, and once past the cottages (spot the WHS initials on the cottages which stand for W H Smith) turn left for 100m and then fork half-right up Reservoir Hill as the trees on the left fall away. Continue up through **Great Wood**, heading north-westwards for 1.4km. The route through the woods is mostly straight (with

Round House to the north of Fawley

white arrows painted on trees), with a slight dogleg in the middle; ignore all side routes. Emerge from the wood and continue along the enclosed bridleway, later going to the left of a house and passing a seat with a view. Continue along the driveway towards **Roundhouse Farm**, passing the 16th-century Pink Cottage and the unusual 18th-century Round House.

Turn right along the minor road for 275m, and just before the right-hand bend go left down an enclosed path with a house on the right. Continue down through the trees, cross the track and stile and head uphill, following a line of wooden electricity poles to a stile. Keep straight on (west) along the track towards **Bosmore Farm**, pass a gate and continue along the surfaced drive to pass some buildings and another gate. Turn right (north) at the junction, following the drive past Bosmore Farmhouse. Continue along the drive past a pond (left) and keep left (straight on) at the split. At the end of the drive, just after the large house (left), turn left through a gate and go through trees to another gate. Continue across the field and then go half-right across the next field to a stile, aiming just right of the buildings.

Turn left down the lane for 150m and then turn right along the entrance drive towards Coxlease Farm for 100m. Fork left, go through a gate and follow the enclosed track (the route now follows this track southwards for 1.3km, with some lovely views ahead and to the right across the Stonor Valley). On entering a field bear right alongside the hedge, go down to a stile and enter Paradise Wood before turning left, heading downhill. Leave

map continues opposite.

194

View across the Stonor Valley after Coxlease Farm

the trees and keep right to enter a field and head diagonally (south-south-east) down to a gate.

Turn left along the road (B480) for 475m to **Middle Assendon** and just after passing The Rainbow pub turn left along the road for Fawley for 75m. After the last house on the right, turn right up along the Oxfordshire Way (the route now follows this trail back to Henley-on-Thames). Follow the fence uphill through the trees to a stile; keep ahead through the field, heading east to another stile, and then go between fences. Cross the corner of a field and continue between fences to a minor road. Cross over and take the track opposite, past Pond Cottage.

Following the Oxfordshire Way over No Man's Hill after passing Henley Park

Follow this track for 1km, later the track is surfaced and passes **Henley Park**.

At the sharp left bend go straight on past a gate and head south-east through the long field over **No Man's Hill** for 1km, following the **Oxfordshire Way** towards The Mount. Later start descending, go through a gate and keep ahead through the wood for 175m. Continue down the enclosed path to the road (A4130) and turn left towards **Henley-on-Thames**. Go straight on at two round-abouts, following the A4130, and turn left along New Street, passing the former Brakspear Brewery. Bear right alongside the River Thames to return to the crossroads beside the bridge. (To reach the railway station from the bridge, continue straight on along Thameside, keep beside the river at the first junction and soon bear right onto Station Road and take the second left to the station.)

WALK 33
South and North Stoke and Grim's Ditch

Start/finish	Junction of Ridgeway and minor road, 1km south of the A4130 east of Crowmarsh Gifford (SU 635 875); limited parking
Distance	15.2km (9½ miles)
Ascent	135m
Time	4hrs
Map	OS Explorer 171
Refreshments	Perch and Pike Inn (01491 872415) and shop at South Stoke
Public transport	South Stoke has bus links to Goring and Wallingford; Buses to Reading and Oxford stop on the A4130 near Mongewell Park (SU 612 881)

This fairly long, but mostly level, walk explores the open landscape to be found along the western fringes of the Chiltern Hills. The route heads across open fields to South Stoke before following a peaceful stretch of the River Thames northwards to pass through North Stoke and arrive at Mongewell. After an optional visit to an interesting partially ruined church, the final section follows the ancient earthwork of Grim's Ditch back to the start.

Follow the minor road south for 700m past some houses and down to a T-junction. Cross over and follow the **Icknield Way** (bridleway) between hedges and then fields for 1.2km, passing east of **Coblers Hill**. Cross the minor road, follow the path to the left of the driveway past **Larkstoke Stud** and continue between hedges. Cross another minor road and continue through the trees, passing left of a stone monument before crossing the field to a hedge gap. With care, cross the A4074 diagonally left, head up the bank and go through a hedge gap, continue across the field to a cross-junction with a bridleway. Turn right, still following **Swan's Way**, and go up to

*The Perch and Pike
at South Stoke*

the trees and a cross-path junction on **Watch Folly**. Turn half-left (south-west) to go across the fields for 1.3km before bearing right along the minor road (Woodcote Road) to reach a crossroads at **South Stoke**.

Cross over and turn left along the **B4009** for 200m, then go right down Cross Keys Road (village shop on right). Pass under the railway bridge to reach a T-junction and turn right along The Street, soon passing the 17th-century red-brick and flint Perch and Pike Inn and St Andrew's Church (the walk now follows The Ridgeway National Trail back to the start).

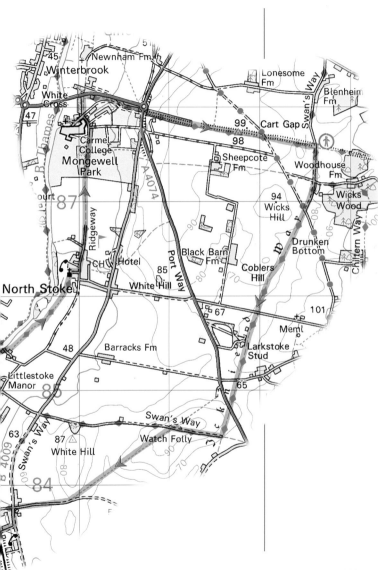

By the time of the Domesday Book the little **village** of **South Stoke** had been given to the Bishop of Lincoln and was known as Bishopstoke; however, soon after it was transferred to Eynsham Abbey and became known as Stoke Abbas. The abbey owned the village until the dissolution of the monasteries in 1539, and in 1546 Henry VIII gave South Stoke to Christ Church in Oxford. Much of the surrounding land is still in their ownership.

St Andrew's Church, which dates from the early 13th century, contains some interesting memorials, including one to Dr Griffiths Higgs (1589–1659) – formerly Chaplain to Queen Elizabeth of Bohemia and Dean of Lichfield – who founded an educational charity that continues today.

Following the Ridgeway alongside the peaceful River Thames between South and North Stoke

At the junction go left along Ferry Lane and keep left at the next junction to reach the **River Thames** opposite **Moulsford**.

Moulsford Viaduct

At one time a ferry gave access to Moulsford and the **pub** is named after a type of mallet (beetle) used to hammer the wedge for splitting logs that were floated down the river. H G Wells used the pub as a model for the Potwell Inn in his novel *The History of Mr Polly*.

Turn right through the gate and follow the peaceful riverside path (on the opposite bank is the Church of St John the Baptist). Pass under the unusual twin-skewed multi-arched brick viaducts. ▶

Continue alongside the river, later crossing a foot-bridge beside a WWII pillbox. Shortly turn right, going away from the river and towards some buildings, and then left along an enclosed path to a gate. Continue through three fields and then along the enclosed path, passing through gates to enter the churchyard at **North Stoke**. Continue past the church and leave through the lychgate.

These were built in the 19th century to carry Isambard Kingdom Brunel's Great Western Railway, which linked London to Bristol, across the River Thames.

201

*Sundial on the side of
North Stoke's church*

The Church of St Mary the Virgin in **North Stoke** was built around 1230 when Robert de Esthall was the rector (his memorial slab is located in the chancel floor). The oak chest is claimed to be a 13th-century crusader chest; Earl Richard of Cornwall, who had links with the church, was in Palestine between 1236 and 1242. The most notable features are the 14th-century wall paintings, which include the Martyrdom of St Stephen and The Last Supper.

Famous residents of North Stoke have included the concert singer Dame Clara Butt (1872–1936), who is buried in the churchyard; the actor Michael Caine; and Deep Purple's vocalist Ian Gillan, who had a guitar-shaped swimming pool built in the grounds of his Victorian Tudor-style home – now the Springs Hotel on the Wallingford Road.

Go along Church Lane and turn left at the T-junction, soon passing the unusual village hall and then the Mill House. Keep straight along the tree-lined bridleway past the golf course, heading north towards **Mongewell Park** for 1.2km.

Mongewell Park, once the home of Shute Barrington (1734–1826), Bishop of Durham, was rebuilt in 1890 for Alexander Frazer in a 'William and Mary' style. Following its use during both world wars, the park became the home of the Carmel College (a Jewish boarding school) until 1997; previous pupils included the film director Roland Joffe (*The Killing Fields* and *The Mission*) and Sir Philip Green, one of Britain's wealthiest men. The site is now awaiting redevelopment. Agatha Christie, who lived at nearby Winterbrook, is said to have used the park as inspiration for the mansion in *The Mousetrap* – the world's longest-running play.

Continue along the surfaced track past buildings and keep ahead at the junction with Judge's Ride, soon passing a small lake and houses to reach a right-hand bend.

The 'man of sensibility' in St John's Church, Mongewell

Detour to St John's Church

Go left along the surfaced track, fork right and soon bear left through a gate just before some private buildings. Retrace your steps back to the main route (400m return).

The partially ruined **church** dates back to Norman times, although the slender brick tower dates from Shute Barrington's Gothic restoration in the late 18th century. Inside are two early 18th-century

Heading east along the ancient earthwork of Grim's Ditch, seen here at Cart Gap

monuments, including one with an effigy of 'a man of sensibility' dressed in Eastern costume and a turban.

Go straight on along the enclosed bridleway (Ridgeway) towards the A4130, and just before the underpass turn right. Follow the path parallel to the A4130 and soon pass through the fence on the right, before continuing through the trees to a gate. With care cross over the **A4074** and turn right for 25m, then left; go through the gate and up a short rise. The route now follows Grim's Ditch – a ridge stretching from the River Thames to Nuffield – for 2km back to the start, passing a trig point and crossing a minor road at **Cart Gap** on the way to end at another minor road.

WALK 34

Goring-on-Thames and Cray's Pond

Start/finish	Goring and Streatley railway station in Goring-on-Thames, near junction of B4526 and B4009 (SU 602 806); parking available nearby
Distance	13.6km (8½ miles) or 8.9km (5½ miles)
Ascent	305m or 190m
Time	4hrs or 2½hrs
Map	OS Explorer 171
Refreshments	Catherine Wheel (01491 872379), The John Barleycorn (01491 872509), Miller of Mansfield (01491 872829) and cafés and shops in Goring-on-Thames
Public transport	Trains to Goring and Streatley station; bus services from Wallingford and Reading

From Goring-on-Thames the walk follows a section of the Thames Path, alongside the peaceful River Thames, before heading up past Hartslock Nature Reserve for a great view. From here the route heads through woods and open fields to visit Cold Harbour and Cray's Pond. The final section passes Elvendon Priory before dropping back down to Goring-on-Thames, following a section of the Chiltern Way. A shorter route, missing out Cray's Pond, is also described.

Leave the station from platform 4 and turn left along Gatehampton Road, then go left again across the bridge. Turn left along Red Cross Road and then right down Station Road Road (or use the footbridge to exit the west side of the station and then follow Station Road westwards), later passing the car park entrance and The Catherine Wheel pub (Manor Road on the left has road-side parking). Follow the road as it curves right past The John Barleycorn, and shortly turn left on a surfaced path towards the **church**. (Ahead is The Miller of Mansfield pub.) Continue through the churchyard (church on left), leave through a gate in the far-right corner and bear right

GORING-ON-THAMES

Goring-on-Thames, along with neighbouring Streatley, is situated in the Goring Gap, where the River Thames flows between the Chilterns and the Berkshire Downs. This has been a major crossing point over the Thames for centuries (the ancient Icknield Way crossed here), although the first bridge wasn't built until 1837, quickly followed by the opening of Isambard Kingdom Brunel's famous Great Western Railway, linking London with Bristol, which passes through the gap.

The Norman church of St Thomas of Canterbury was probably built by Robert d'Oilly, a Norman baron and staunch supporter of William the Conqueror, who held 60 manors including 'Garinges' (Goring). The church features a bell cast in 1290 – believed to be one of the oldest in Britain – while the wooden rood screen is carved out of oak from HMS Thunderer, a bomb-ketch that fought under Nelson at the Battle of Trafalgar.

along the lane to a junction. Turn left to the **River Thames**, passing the watermill, and turn left again.

Follow the Thames Path downstream for 3km, later passing under the brick viaduct built to take Isambard Kingdom Brunel's Great Western Railway across the river. Just before Ferry Cottage turn left, away from the river; go between paddocks to a T-junction and then go right for 600m, still following the Thames Path.

At Hartslock Wood turn left and head uphill, then go through

a gate and follow the right-hand fence to a seat with a view to the west of the River Thames and Gatehampton Viaduct with the Berkshire Downs beyond. Continue down alongside the fence through Hartslock Nature Reserve to a gate at the corner.

Take a short detour through Hartslock Nature Reserve for an even better view to the west

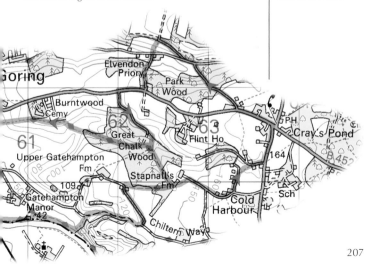

This BBOWT **nature reserve** is home to a range of plants, including the rare monkey orchid, which typically flowers during May. A permissive path (gate on right after the seat; see the information board) leads through the reserve to an excellent viewpoint (400m return).

Go through the gate and turn right, following the shaded route uphill for 700m. Fork left at the sign and bear left along the surfaced track (**Chiltern Way**) as it quickly bends left towards **Upper Gatehampton Farm**. Follow the track as it curves right beside a farm building and as the track swings left fork right, following the Chiltern Way between the fence (left) and trees. Head east through **Great Chalk Wood** for 450m to a junction in a dip.

Shortcut

For the shorter walk, turn left (Chiltern Way) down through the trees to reach a junction at SU 623 803. Rejoin the main walk by turning left.

Keep ahead up to a track at **Stapnall's Farm** and bear right then right again, following the surfaced track south-eastwards. Keep ahead (left) at the junction, following the surfaced track as it curves left through **Cold Harbour**. Keep left at the next junction and continue for 200m before turning half-right through a gate. Head north-east across two fields and down to some houses. Turn right up the surfaced drive and then left alongside the road (B471) to the crossroads at **Cray's Pond**. The pond is on your right. Cross over and turn left, following the road towards Goring-on-Thames for 400m.

Turn right along a track (signposted Icknield Way 1¾), later heading down through **Park Wood**. Later to your left is **Elvendon Priory**.

This former religious **site** was probably established during the 11th century, although the present (private) building, which has been extensively re-built, dates from the 15th century.

Cross the minor road and turn left for 100m. Fork right past a gate and follow the track uphill to a crossing path. Turn left through a gate and go diagonally right down across the field to another gate. Cross the minor road and follow the enclosed path opposite (signposted 'Park Farm ¼'). Continue up the surfaced drive (look back for a view of Elvendon Priory) for 250m and pass between the buildings at Park Farm. Turn right along the road (B4526) for 300m, then turn left across the road to follow a bridleway southwards. Follow the track as it soon bears left, keeping near the top of **Great Chalk Wood**.

Where the track curves right, keep ahead (left) beside the hedge to reach a bridleway junction. Fork right for 125m up to another junction (SU 623 803 – the shortcut rejoins here) and turn right; the walk now follows the Chiltern Way back to Goring-on-Thames. Afer 50m fork right, soon cross a tack, and head generally west-north-west through the wood, later keeping right at a split and heading down to a gate. Follow the right-hand field edge through the open access land and

Messing about on the River Thames at Goring Lock

Gatehampton Viaduct

leave through another gate; bear right up the field edge and then left at the top. Follow the right-hand boundary through the next field down to the corner and turn half-right across the sports field towards the houses in **Goring-on-Thames**. Go through the hedge to the housing estate (Whitehills Green) and follow the road ahead, then go left and right before turning left down the main road to a junction with Gatehampton Road. Turn left for the **station**, or, to reach the car park, turn right and follow the first part of the walk.

WALK 35

Whitchurch Hill and Mapledurham

Start/finish	Roadside parking along Hill Bottom, Whitchurch Hill, near the junction with Bridle Road and Gashes Lane, 200m north-west of The Sun (SU 641 793)
Distance	12.1km (7½ miles)
Ascent	275m
Time	3½hrs
Maps	OS Explorer 171
Refreshments	The Sun (0118 9842260) at Whitchurch Hill
Public transport	Bus links (excluding Sundays) to Whitchurch Hill from Reading and Goring

This walk explores the lovely beech woods and open farmland to the north of the River Thames. Along the way there is a great viewpoint and the opportunity to take a look around Mapledurham with its historic house, mill and church. The village has starred in a number of big-screen and TV productions.

Head east-south-east through Hill Bottom, passing The Sun pub to reach a road junction. Turn left (Goring Heath) and continue for 150m, crossing the road on the way, and then turn right along a hedge-lined track, heading southwards for 600m. Go through a gate on the left and follow the left-hand side of the field towards **Path Hill** for 200m. (The walk now follows the Chiltern Way to Mapledurham.) Go through a gate and keep ahead past a house before bearing left along the minor road to reach a junction where you turn right. Follow the lane as it bends left, and at a right-hand bend fork left and go down through the trees (signposted Collins End ½). Continue down across the field to a dip, passing a tree, keep ahead for 25m and bear diagonally right to go up past some bushes with an old fence on the right.

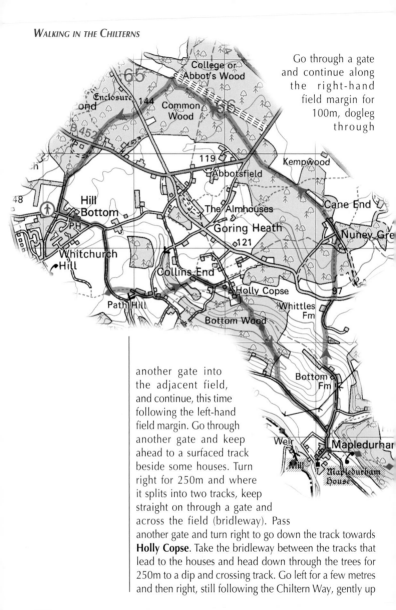

Go through a gate and continue along the right-hand field margin for 100m, dogleg through

another gate into the adjacent field, and continue, this time following the left-hand field margin. Go through another gate and keep ahead to a surfaced track beside some houses. Turn right for 250m and where it splits into two tracks, keep straight on through a gate and across the field (bridleway). Pass another gate and turn right to go down the track towards **Holly Copse**. Take the bridleway between the tracks that lead to the houses and head down through the trees for 250m to a dip and crossing track. Go left for a few metres and then right, still following the Chiltern Way, gently up through **Bottom Wood**. After 450m Ignore a permissive path on the right and go straight on. Go through a gate and keep ahead to a seat.

MAPLEDURHAM

The water mill at Mapledurham

The secluded and appealing riverside hamlet of Mapledurham has a number of 17th-century cottages lining its single street, while at its far end, down a short track on the right, is the 15th-century mill – the oldest working water-mill on the Thames – where you can still buy flour. To the left is St Margaret's Church, built around 1200 and notable for its screened-off Catholic chapel that dates from the late 1300s. The chapel now belongs to the Eystons, heirs of the Blount family, the traditional Catholic owners of the Mapledurham estate. Parts of Mapledurham House date from the 15th century, although most of what is seen today is the result of rebuilding by Sir Michael Blount in 1588.

The village was used as the location for the film *The Eagle has Landed*, in which it was known as 'Studley Constable' and based in Norfolk (the Spyglass and Kettle pub was a fake – there is no pub in the village). It has also starred in numerous TV dramas, including *The Forsyte Saga*, *The Wind in the Willows* and *Inspector Morse*. The house, tea-shop and mill are open to the public – for opening times call 0118 972 3350.

Take a moment to admire the **views**: to the south-east you can see Mapledurham House, with the church in Purley-on-Thames just across the River Thames. Further on is the wind turbine at Reading, while to the south-west are the North Hampshire Downs and the communications mast on Cottington's Hill, 25km away.

Head south, going steeply downhill, then go through a gate and turn left along the enclosed bridleway to join a minor road beside a cottage (SU 671 770). To visit Mapledurham turn right, soon passing some houses (including the old Almshouses), and arrive at the church. Beyond is **Mapledurham House** and to your right is the watermill.

After visiting Mapledurham the walk heads along the valley past Bottom Farm

Retrace your steps back past the cottage (SU 671 770) and continue northwards along the lane, turning left at the corner and following the surfaced track towards **Bottom Farm** (signposted 'Goring Heath 1½'). After passing some cottages (right) turn right and go up through

three fields. Before the field corner go through a gate on the right and turn left along the track past **Whittles Farm**. Cross the road slightly to the right, go through a gate and follow the left-hand field edge. Keep ahead through the trees of Nuney Wood, later with a fence on your left. Go through a gate and turn left along the track at **Nuney Green**, keeping straight on at the junction and heading north-westwards to where the track splits to two cottages. Keep ahead on the enclosed bridleway between the two tracks to enter a wood. Soon pass between two small ponds, doglegging left-right to follow a fence on the right. Keep ahead at a staggered cross-path junction, with the edge of the wood on your right, to reach Deadman's Lane (B4526).

Cross over, head north-west through Bensgrove Wood (bridleway) for 500m and then bear left at the split to a track. (There are a number of paths through this section – keep a lookout for the white arrows on the trees.) Turn right, ignoring a path to the left after 75m and follow the fence on the left; keep ahead at the cross-junction, following the bridleway north-westwards to another cross-junction. Turn left (south-west), staying in **Common Wood**, to reach a minor road after 500m. Cross over and follow the bridleway (signposted 'Whitchurch Hill 1½') ahead through the trees for 600m to reach a road (B4526).

Cross over, pass a gate and follow the track for 150m before bearing slightly left on a narrower bridleway through the trees of Great Oaks. After leaving the wood keep ahead, following a track (Gashes Lane), later with buildings on the left, to return to **Hill Bottom**.

APPENDIX A

Route summary table

No	Start/finish	OS grid ref	Distance km (miles)	Ascent (m)	Time (hrs)	Page
North of Luton						
1	Harlington	TL 037 304	9.2 (5¾)	175	2½	24
2	Barton-le-Clay	TL 085 304	15.7 or 10.9 (9¾ or 6¾)	250 or 170	4½ or 3	29
3	Pirton	TL 145 315	10.9 (6¾)	240	3¼	35
Dunstable to Berkhamsted						
4	Whipsnade	TL 009 180	16.1 or 8 (10 or 5)	325, 130 or 195	5 or 2½	42
5	Pitstone Hill	SP 954 149	13 or 8.4 (8 or 5¼)	300 or 215	3¾ or 2½	48
6	Tring Station	SP 950 122	11.9 (7½)	305	3½	53
7	Tring Station	SP 948 120	12.8 (8)	230	3½	57
8	Great Gaddesden	TL 029 112	7.5 (4¾)	110	2	62
9	Berkhamsted	SP 993 081	16.9 or 12.5 (10½ or 7¾)	370 or 290	5 or 3½	67
Wendover to Stokenchurch						
10	Cholesbury	SP 931 071	8.1 (5)	200	2½	74
11	Wendover	SP 869 078	14.1 (8¾)	340	4¼	78
12	Wendover	SP 869 078	12 (7½)	295	3½	85
13	Whiteleaf Hill	SP 822 036	8 (5)	250	2½	90
14	Chinnor Hill	SP 766 002	12.8 (8)	420	4	95
15	Lacey Green	SP 818 006	12.1 (7½)	295	3½	101
16	Great Hampden	SP 847 013	8.7 (5½)	185	2½	106
17	Great Missenden	SP 895 014	13.8 or 10.5 (8½ or 6½)	270 or 175	4 or 3	110

No	Start/finish	OS grid ref	Distance km (miles)	Ascent (m)	Time (hrs)	Page
Amersham to High Wycombe						
18	Little Chalfont	TQ 004 982	8.8 or 10.3 (5½ or 6½)	150 or 160	2½ or 3	118
19	Amersham Old Town	SU 947 978	12.1 or 8.4 (7½ or 5¼)	165 or 130	3½ or 2½	123
20	Hughenden	SU 864 955	13 (8)	395	4	128
21	Penn and Tylers Green	SU 907 937	13 or 6.9 (8 or 4¼)	255 or 160	3¾ or 2	133
Watlington and Nettlebed						
22	Cowleaze Wood	SU 725 956	13.3 (8¼)	410	4	140
23	Turville	SU 767 911	11.3 or 5.5 (7 or 3½)	480 or 230	3¾ or 1¾	145
24	Pishill	SU 726 898	9.5 (6)	320	3	150
25	Pishill	SU 726 898	14.3 or 10 (9 or 6¼)	410 or 335	4¼ or 3	155
26	Ewelme	SU 648 911	11.6 (7¼)	310	3½	160
27	Checkendon	SU 663 830	12 (7½)	300	3½	165
28	Grim's Ditch, Ipsden	SU 635 875	9.5 (6)	210	2¾	170
29	Nettlebed	SU 701 867	14.6 or 12.8 (9 or 8)	310 or 235	4 or 3½	173
30	Greys Green	SU 720 829	7.2 (4½)	130	2	179
Along the Thames						
31	Mill End	SU 785 854	13.6 (8½)	270	3¾	184
32	Henley-on-Thames	SU 763 826	18.5 (11½)	375	5½	190
33	Grim's Ditch, Ipsden	SU 635 875	15.2 (9½)	135	4	197
34	Goring-on-Thames	SU 602 806	13.6 or 8.9 (8½ or 5½)	305 or 190	4 or 2½	205
35	Hill Bottom	SU 641 793	12.1 (7½)	275	3½	211

APPENDIX B
Useful contacts

For up-to-date information on the Chilterns AONB, accommodation and other visitor information, contact www.chilternsaonb.org or the tourist information offices listed below.

Chilterns AONB
01844 355500
www.chilternsaonb.org

Chiltern Society
01494 771250
www.chilternsociety.org.uk

Tourist information
Visit Buckinghamshire
www.visitbuckinghamshire.org

Visit Chilterns
www.visitchilterns.co.uk

Visit Southern Oxfordshire
www.southernoxfordshire.com

Local Tourist Information Offices
Dunstable
01582 891420

Goring-on-Thames
01491 873565

Henley-on-Thames
01491 578034

Tring
01442 823347

Wallingford
01491 826972

Public transport information
For train enquiries contact
National Rail:
08457 484950
www.nationalrail.co.uk

Traveline is the best resource for checking bus timetables:
0871 2002233
www.traveline.info

Local wildlife trusts
Bedfordshire, Cambridgeshire and Northamptonshire Wildlife Trust
01954 713500
www.wildlifebcn.org

Berkshire, Buckinghamshire and Oxfordshire Wildlife Trust (BBOWT)
01865 775476
www.bbowt.org.uk

Hertfordshire and Middlesex Wildlife Trust
01727 858901
www.hertswildlifetrust.org.uk

Other contacts
English Heritage
0370 333 1181
www.english-heritage.org.uk

National Trust
0344 800 1895
www.nationaltrust.org.uk

Ramblers Association
020 7339 8500
www.ramblers.org.uk

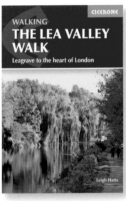
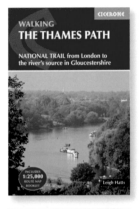
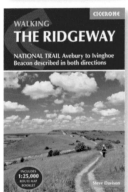
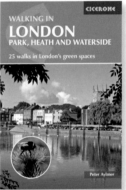

LISTING OF CICERONE GUIDES

SCOTLAND

Backpacker's Britain: Northern
    Scotland
Ben Nevis and Glen Coe
Cycling in the Hebrides
Great Mountain Days in Scotland
Mountain Biking in Southern and
    Central Scotland
Mountain Biking in West and North
    West Scotland
Not the West Highland Way
Scotland
Scotland's Best Small Mountains
Scotland's Far West
Scotland's Mountain Ridges
Scrambles in Lochaber
The Ayrshire and Arran Coastal
    Paths
The Border Country
The Cape Wrath Trail
The Great Glen Way
The Great Glen Way Map Booklet
The Hebridean Way
The Hebrides
The Isle of Mull
The Isle of Skye
The Skye Trail
The Southern Upland Way
The Speyside Way
The Speyside Way Map Booklet
The West Highland Way
Walking Highland Perthshire
Walking in Scotland's Far North
Walking in the Angus Glens
Walking in the Cairngorms
Walking in the Ochils, Campsie
    Fells and Lomond Hills
Walking in the Pentland Hills
Walking in the Southern Uplands
Walking in Torridon
Walking Loch Lomond and the
    Trossachs
Walking on Arran
Walking on Harris and Lewis
Walking on Jura, Islay and
    Colonsay
Walking on Rum and the Small Isles
Walking on the Orkney and
    Shetland Isles
Walking on Uist and Barra
Walking the Corbetts
    Vol 1 South of the Great Glen
Walking the Corbetts
    Vol 2 North of the Great Glen
Walking the Galloway Hills
Walking the Munros
    Vol 1 – Southern, Central and
    Western Highlands

Walking the Munros
    Vol 2 – Northern Highlands and
    the Cairngorms
West Highland Way Map Booklet
Winter Climbs Ben Nevis and
    Glen Coe
Winter Climbs in the Cairngorms

NORTHERN ENGLAND TRAILS

Hadrian's Wall Path
Hadrian's Wall Path Map Booklet
Pennine Way Map Booklet
The Coast to Coast Map Booklet
The Coast to Coast Walk
The Dales Way
The Dales Way Map Booklet
The Pennine Way

LAKE DISTRICT

Cycling in the Lake District
Great Mountain Days in the Lake
    District
Lake District Winter Climbs
Lake District: High Level and Fell
    Walks
Lake District: Low Level and Lake
    Walks
Lakeland Fellranger
Mountain Biking in the Lake District
Scrambles in the Lake District –
    North and South
Short Walks in Lakeland Book 1:
    South Lakeland
Short Walks in Lakeland Book 2:
    North Lakeland
Short Walks in Lakeland Book 3:
    West Lakeland
Tour of the Lake District
Trail and Fell Running in the Lake
    District

NORTH WEST ENGLAND AND
THE ISLE OF MAN

Cycling the Pennine Bridleway
Cycling the Way of the Roses
Isle of Man Coastal Path
The Lancashire Cycleway
The Lune Valley and Howgills
The Ribble Way
Walking in Cumbria's Eden Valley
Walking in Lancashire
Walking in the Forest of Bowland
    and Pendle
Walking on the Isle of Man
Walking on the West Pennine
    Moors
Walks in Lancashire Witch Country
Walks in Ribble Country
Walks in Silverdale and Arnside

NORTH EAST ENGLAND,
YORKSHIRE DALES AND
PENNINES

Cycling in the Yorkshire Dales
Great Mountain Days in the
    Pennines
Mountain Biking in the Yorkshire
    Dales
South Pennine Walks
St Oswald's Way and St Cuthbert's
    Way
The Cleveland Way and the
    Yorkshire Wolds Way
The Cleveland Way Map Booklet
The North York Moors
The Reivers Way
The Teesdale Way
Walking in County Durham
Walking in Northumberland
Walking in the North Pennines
Walking in the Yorkshire Dales:
    North and East
Walking in the Yorkshire Dales:
    South and West
Walks in Dales Country
Walks in the Yorkshire Dales

WALES AND WELSH BORDERS

Glyndwr's Way
Great Mountain Days in Snowdonia
Hillwalking in Shropshire
Hillwalking in Wales – Vol 1
Hillwalking in Wales – Vol 2
Mountain Walking in Snowdonia
Offa's Dyke Path
Offa's Dyke Map Booklet
Pembrokeshire Coast Path Map
    Booklet
Ridges of Snowdonia
Scrambles in Snowdonia
The Ascent of Snowdon
The Ceredigion and Snowdonia
    Coast Paths
The Pembrokeshire Coast Path
The Severn Way
The Snowdonia Way
The Wales Coast Path
The Wye Valley Walk
Walking in Carmarthenshire
Walking in Pembrokeshire
Walking in the Forest of Dean
Walking in the South Wales Valleys
Walking in the Wye Valley
Walking on the Brecon Beacons
Walking on the Gower
Welsh Winter Climbs

DERBYSHIRE, PEAK DISTRICT AND MIDLANDS

Cycling in the Peak District
Dark Peak Walks
Scrambles in the Dark Peak
Walking in Derbyshire
White Peak Walks: The Northern Dales
White Peak Walks: The Southern Dales

SOUTHERN ENGLAND

20 Classic Sportive Rides in South East England
20 Classic Sportive Rides in South West England
Cycling in the Cotswolds
Mountain Biking on the North Downs
Mountain Biking on the South Downs
North Downs Way Map Booklet
South West Coast Path Map Booklet – Minehead to St Ives
South West Coast Path Map Booklet – Plymouth to Poole
South West Coast Path Map Booklet – St Ives to Plymouth
Suffolk Coast and Heath Walks
The Cotswold Way
The Cotswold Way Map Booklet
The Great Stones Way
The Kennet and Avon Canal
The Lea Valley Walk
The North Downs Way
The Peddars Way and Norfolk Coast Path
The Pilgrims' Way
The Ridgeway Map Booklet
The Ridgeway National Trail
The South Downs Way
The South Downs Way Map Booklet
The South West Coast Path
The Thames Path
The Thames Path Map Booklet
The Two Moors Way
Walking Hampshire's Test Way
Walking in Cornwall
Walking in Essex
Walking in Kent
Walking in London
Walking in Norfolk
Walking in Sussex
Walking in the Chilterns
Walking in the Cotswolds
Walking in the Isles of Scilly
Walking in the New Forest
Walking in the North Wessex Downs
Walking in the Thames Valley
Walking on Dartmoor
Walking on Guernsey
Walking on Jersey
Walking on the Isle of Wight
Walking the Jurassic Coast
Walks in the South Downs National Park

BRITISH ISLES CHALLENGES, COLLECTIONS AND ACTIVITIES

The Book of the Bivvy
The Book of the Bothy
The C2C Cycle Route
The End to End Cycle Route
The Mountains of England and Wales: Vol 1 Wales
The Mountains of England and Wales: Vol 2 England
The National Trails
The UK's County Tops
Three Peaks, Ten Tors

ALPS CROSS-BORDER ROUTES

100 Hut Walks in the Alps
Across the Eastern Alps: E5
Alpine Ski Mountaineering Vol 1 – Western Alps
Alpine Ski Mountaineering Vol 2 – Central and Eastern Alps
Chamonix to Zermatt
The Karnischer Höhenweg
The Tour of the Bernina
Tour of Mont Blanc
Tour of Monte Rosa
Tour of the Matterhorn
Trail Running – Chamonix and the Mont Blanc region
Trekking in the Alps
Trekking in the Silvretta and Rätikon Alps
Trekking Munich to Venice
Walking in the Alps

PYRENEES AND FRANCE/SPAIN CROSS-BORDER ROUTES

The GR10 Trail
The GR11 Trail
The Pyrenean Haute Route
The Pyrenees
The Way of St James – Spain
Walks and Climbs in the Pyrenees

AUSTRIA

The Adlerweg
Trekking in Austria's Hohe Tauern
Trekking in the Stubai Alps
Trekking in the Zillertal Alps
Walking in Austria

SWITZERLAND

Cycle Touring in Switzerland
The Swiss Alpine Pass Route – Via Alpina Route 1
The Swiss Alps
Tour of the Jungfrau Region
Walking in the Bernese Oberland
Walking in the Valais
Walks in the Engadine – Switzerland

FRANCE AND BELGIUM

Chamonix Mountain Adventures
Cycle Touring in France
Cycling London to Paris
Cycling the Canal du Midi
Écrins National Park
Mont Blanc Walks
Mountain Adventures in the Maurienne
The GR20 Corsica
The GR5 Trail
The GR5 Trail – Vosges and Jura
The Grand Traverse of the Massif Central
The Loire Cycle Route
The Moselle Cycle Route
The River Rhone Cycle Route
The Robert Louis Stevenson Trail
The Way of St James
Tour of the Oisans: The GR54
Tour of the Queyras
Tour of the Vanoise
Vanoise Ski Touring
Via Ferratas of the French Alps
Walking in Corsica
Walking in Provence – East
Walking in Provence – West
Walking in the Auvergne
Walking in the Briançonnais
Walking in the Cevennes
Walking in the Dordogne
Walking in the Haute Savoie: North
Walking in the Haute Savoie: South
Walks in the Cathar Region
Walking in the Ardennes

GERMANY

Hiking and Biking in the Black Forest
The Danube Cycleway Volume 1
The Rhine Cycle Route
The Westweg
Walking in the Bavarian Alps

ICELAND AND GREENLAND

Trekking in Greenland
Walking and Trekking in Iceland

IRELAND

The Irish Coast to Coast Walk
The Mountains of Ireland
The Wild Atlantic Way and
    Western Ireland

ITALY

Italy's Sibillini National Park
Shorter Walks in the Dolomites
Ski Touring and Snowshoeing in the
    Dolomites
The Way of St Francis
Through the Italian Alps
Trekking in the Apennines
Trekking in the Dolomites
Via Ferratas of the Italian Dolomites
    Vol 1
Via Ferratas of the Italian
    Dolomites: Vol 2
Walking and Trekking in the Gran
    Paradiso
Walking in Abruzzo
Walking in Italy's Stelvio National
    Park
Walking in Sardinia
Walking in Sicily
Walking in the Dolomites
Walking in Tuscany
Walking in Umbria
Walking on the Amalfi Coast
Walking the Italian Lakes
Walks and Treks in the Maritime
    Alps

SCANDINAVIA: NORWAY, SWEDEN, FINLAND

Walking in Norway

EASTERN EUROPE AND THE BALKANS

The Danube Cycleway Volume 2
The High Tatras
The Mountains of Romania
Walking in Bulgaria's National
    Parks
Walking in Hungary
Mountain Biking in Slovenia
The Islands of Croatia
The Julian Alps of Slovenia
The Mountains of Montenegro
The Peaks of the Balkans Trail
Trekking in Slovenia
Walking in Croatia
Walking in Slovenia: The
    Karavanke

SPAIN

Coastal Walks in Andalucia
Cycle Touring in Spain
Mountain Walking in Mallorca
Mountain Walking in Southern
    Catalunya
Spain's Sendero Histórico: The GR1
The Andalucian Coast to Coast
    Walk
The Mountains of Nerja
The Mountains of Ronda and
    Grazalema
The Northern Caminos
The Sierras of Extremadura
The Way of St James Cyclist Guide
Trekking in Mallorca
Walking and Trekking in the Sierra
    Nevada
Walking in Andalucia
Walking in Menorca
Walking in the Cordillera
    Cantabrica
Walking on Gran Canaria
Walking on La Gomera and El
    Hierro
Walking on La Palma
Walking on Lanzarote and
    Fuerteventura
Walking on Tenerife
Walking on the Costa Blanca

PORTUGAL

The Camino Portugués
Walking in Portugal
Walking in the Algarve

GREECE, CYPRUS AND MALTA

The High Mountains of Crete
Trekking in Greece
Walking and Trekking on Corfu
Walking in Cyprus
Walking on Malta

INTERNATIONAL CHALLENGES, COLLECTIONS AND ACTIVITIES

Canyoning in the Alps
The Via Francigena Canterbury to
    Rome – Parts 1 and 2

AFRICA

Climbing in the Moroccan Anti-
    Atlas
Mountaineering in the Moroccan
    High Atlas
The High Atlas
Trekking in the Atlas Mountains
Kilimanjaro
Walking in the Drakensberg

JORDAN

Jordan – Walks, Treks, Caves,
    Climbs and Canyons
Treks and Climbs in Wadi Rum,
    Jordan

ASIA

Annapurna
Everest: A Trekker's Guide
Trekking in the Himalaya
Trekking in Bhutan
Trekking in Ladakh
The Mount Kailash Trek

USA AND CANADA

British Columbia
The John Muir Trail
The Pacific Crest Trail

ARGENTINA, CHILE AND PERU

Aconcagua and the Southern Andes
Hiking and Biking Peru's Inca Trails
Torres del Paine

TECHNIQUES

Geocaching in the UK
Indoor Climbing
Lightweight Camping
Map and Compass
Outdoor Photography
Polar Exploration
Rock Climbing
Sport Climbing
The Mountain Hut Book

MINI GUIDES

Alpine Flowers
Avalanche!
Navigation
Pocket First Aid and Wilderness
    Medicine
Snow

MOUNTAIN LITERATURE

8000 metres
A Walk in the Clouds
Abode of the Gods
The Pennine Way – the Path, the
    People, the Journey
Unjustifiable Risk?

For full information on all our
guides, books and eBooks,
visit our website:
www.cicerone.co.uk

Walking – Trekking – Mountaineering – Climbing – Cycling

Over 40 years, Cicerone have built up an outstanding collection of over 300 guides, inspiring all sorts of amazing adventures.

Every guide comes from extensive exploration and research by our expert authors, all with a passion for their subjects. They are frequently praised, endorsed and used by clubs, instructors and outdoor organisations.

All our titles can now be bought as **e-books**, **ePubs** and **Kindle** files and we also have an online magazine – **Cicerone Extra** – with features to help cyclists, climbers, walkers and trekkers choose their next adventure, at home or abroad.

Our website shows any **new information** we've had in since a book was published. Please do let us know if you find anything has changed, so that we can publish the latest details. On our **website** you'll also find great ideas and lots of detailed information about what's inside every guide and you can buy **individual routes** from many of them online.

It's easy to keep in touch with what's going on at Cicerone by getting our monthly **free e-newsletter**, which is full of offers, competitions, up-to-date information and topical articles. You can subscribe on our home page and also follow us on **Facebook** and **Twitter** or dip into our **blog**.

Cicerone – the very best guides for exploring the world.

CICERONE

Juniper House, Murley Moss, Oxenholme Road, Kendal, Cumbria LA9 7RL
Tel: 015395 62069 info@cicerone.co.uk
www.cicerone.co.uk